THE SOUL
— *of* —
CHRISTIANITY

Also by Huston Smith

The Purposes of Higher Education

The Search for America (edited)

The World's Religions
(originally titled *The Religions of Man*)

Condemned to Meaning

Forgotten Truth:
The Common Vision of the World's Religions

Beyond the Postmodern Mind

Primordial Truth and Postmodern Theology
(with David Griffin)

Huston Smith: Essays on World Religion

The Illustrated World's Religions

One Nation Under God:
The Triumph of the Native American Church
(edited with Reuben Snake)

Why Religion Matters:
The Fate of the Human Spirit in an Age of Disbelief

Cleansing the Doors of Perception:
The Religious Significance of Entheogenic Plants and Chemicals

Buddhism:
A Concise Introduction
(with Philip Novak)

THE SOUL
— of —
CHRISTIANITY

Restoring the Great Tradition

HUSTON SMITH

HarperSanFrancisco
A Division of HarperCollins*Publishers*

THE SOUL OF CHRISTIANITY: *Restoring the Great Tradition.* Copyright © 2005 by Huston Smith. All rights reserved. Printed in the United States of America. No part of this book may be used or reproduced in any manner whatsoever without written permission except in the case of brief quotations embodied in critical articles and reviews. For information address HarperCollins Publishers, 10 East 53rd Street, New York, NY 10022.

HarperCollins books may be purchased for educational, business, or sales promotional use. For information please write: Special Markets Department, HarperCollins Publishers, 10 East 53rd Street, New York, NY 10022.
HarperCollins Web site: http://www.harpercollins.com

HarperCollins®, 📖®, and HarperSanFrancisco™ are
trademarks of HarperCollins Publishers.

FIRST EDITION
Designed by Joseph Rutt

Library of Congress Cataloging-in-Publication Data

Smith, Huston.
    The soul of christianity : restoring the great tradition / Huston Smith.
        p. cm.
    ISBN-13: 978–0–06–079478–1
    ISBN-10: 0–06–079478–X
    1. Christianity. I. Title.
BR121.3.S65 2005
230—dc22   2005046082

05 06 07 08 09 RRD(H) 10 9 8 7 6 5 4 3 2 1

CONTENTS

———◆———

PREFACE   vii

PROLOGUE   xi

INTRODUCTION   xv

Part One
THE CHRISTIAN WORLDVIEW   1

Part Two
THE CHRISTIAN STORY   37

Part Three
THE THREE MAIN BRANCHES OF
CHRISTIANITY TODAY   129

CODA   163

ACKNOWLEDGMENTS   167

INDEX   169

PREFACE

———•——

This is a passionate book, written with a great sense of urgency. Endowed by blood and birth with an instinctive feeling for the holy, a sense of awe for the wonder and beauty of sacred things, I feel like a voice crying in the wilderness, the wilderness of secular modernity which religion is unable to pull us out of because it presents our culture with a babble of conflicting voices. And yet a voice that *can* pull us out of the wilderness is on our very doorstep. That voice is the voice of first-millennium Christianity, the Great Tradition, which all Christians can accept because it is the solid trunk of the tree from which its branches have sprung. It is the voice of peace, justice, and beauty that emanates from the Christian soul and which (in the company of other authentic religions) the world desperately needs.

I am not the only one at work on this project, and among my fellow laborers are a number who are better scholars and theologians than I am. Still, my sense of urgency remains. For precisely *because* of their towering talents it will take time for their thoughts to make their way into our culture. I have tried to write a book which, without oversimplifying, is readily comprehensible to every intelligent reader who is interested.

Several subsidiary points can help to place the book in perspective:

First, it is not a complete account of its subject. It is restricted to Christian *faith* and gives only passing attention to institutional developments, and it bypasses the dark side of Christian history entirely.

Second, it is not a scholarly treatise. It omits references and contains very few footnotes. Here and there I make minor changes in the wordings of the writers I quote so that they will fit smoothly into my text. When quoting scripture I choose whatever translation best suits my needs.

Third, the book is not combative. It respects other interpretations of Christianity and does not argue with them. Their authors have done what they needed to do, and I have done the same.

Last in this list of waivers: while I assume full responsibility for everything through Part One, when I move to the Christian story in Part Two I try not to be innovative. I think of it as the subtitle of the book indicates, as a work of restoration. Countering the current tendency to be skeptical about the past, I try to show how first-millennium Christianity can surprise the present with new life.

Stated positively, I have tried to describe a Christianity which is fully compatible with everything we now know, and to indicate why Christians feel privileged to give their lives to it. I found writing this book exhilarating, for it enabled me to see more clearly than before the intellectual and spiritual gold of Christianity, its intellectual expanse, the vastness of its atmosphere, and its genius for cutting through to the quick of life.

Part One is totally new. Part Two expands and deepens the chapter on Christianity in my book *The World's Religions*. Part Three presents the three main divisions of Christianity today.

PROLOGUE

———

Recently, a former MIT student of mine who went on to became a lifelong friend visited me and told me of an important incident in his life that he realized he had not previously shared.

He was a senior in high school in Cambridge, Massachusetts. Like most teenagers, he had more or less adopted his middle-class parents' outlook, which was atheistic Marxism; and his interests in classical music, literature, and science led him frequently to the Boston Public Library. As he was browsing down one of its corridors one afternoon, his eyes fell on *The Dialogues of Plato.* He had heard of Plato but not read him, so he took the book from its shelf and it opened in his hands to the beginning of the seventh book of *The Republic,* where Plato's most famous passage, the Allegory of the Cave, appears.

Readers of the book in hand will recall that in that allegory Plato asks his readers to imagine people who are imprisoned in a grotto, their legs and necks fettered from childhood so that they remain in the same position, able to look only at the cave's low back wall. Behind them is a bonfire, and between it and the backs of the prisoners is an endless poster parade of men carrying cardboard cutouts of the world's objects. Thus all the prisoners ever see is an ongoing shadow play. Plato then asks us to consider the state of a prisoner who is released from his chains. Turning around, he beholds the bonfire and behind it the grotto's opening. Led (for the prisoner's eyes need to accommodate to the light) out of the cave into broad daylight, he can scarcely believe what he sees: an incredibly beautiful Technicolor world of three dimensions, and presiding over it all the magisterial sun.

Coming to the point of why he was telling me his story, my student said that when he came to the end of Plato's allegory, he found that his face was streaming with tears.

What was it that brought those tears to his eyes? Plato might have said that my student had touched the wellspring of philosophy: the longing to be at home in the world. The Sand People of the Kalahari might say that what he was reading put him in touch with the "big hunger" that lies deeper in the stomach than the "little hunger." For my part, when my student had concluded his visit I found myself flipping to a short passage in my *Why Religion Matters* which reads like this:

There is within us—in even the blithest, most light-hearted among us—a fundamental dis-ease. It acts like an unquenchable fire that renders the vast majority of us incapable in this life of ever coming to full peace. This desire lies in the marrow of our bones and deep in the regions of our soul. All great literature, poetry, art, philosophy, psychology, and religion tries to name and analyze this longing. We are seldom in direct touch with it, and indeed the modern world seems set on preventing us from getting in touch with it by covering it with an unending phantasmagoria of entertainments, obsessions, and distractions of every sort. But the longing is there, built into us like a jack-in-the-box that presses for release. Two great painters suggest this longing in their titles—Gauguin's *Why Are We Here? Where Did We Come From? Where Are We Going?* and de Chirico's *Nostalgia for the Infinite*—but I must work with words. Whether we realize it or not, simply to be human is to long for release from mundane existence with its confining walls of finitude and mortality.

The Good News of authentic religion—in this book, Christianity—is that that longing can be fulfilled.

INTRODUCTION

We live in an exciting time. We are living through the second of the two great revolutions in the human spirit.

The first of these was disastrous for the human spirit, for it pushed it to the margins. The discovery of the controlled experiment in the sixteenth and seventeenth centuries by Galileo, Kepler, and others inaugurated the scientific method, and it quickly displaced the traditional worldview (which pivots on God) with the scientistic worldview, which has no place for deity and is uncompromisingly secular. It's true that religion—in America, primarily Christianity—is all over the map, but that doesn't affect the point here, for cultures are ruled by their mandarins, the intellectuals, and they center in the universities that shape the minds of students who go out to rule the nation. Today's U.S. universities are unreservedly secular.

The second revolution—through which we are now living but which remains undernoticed—is constructive, for it brings

God back into the picture. It is occurring because we now see clearly where secularism went wrong. It equated two things, absence-of-evidence and evidence-of-absence, which, once one stops to think about it, are very different. The fact that science cannot get its hands on anything except nature is no proof that nature (alternatively, matter) is all that exists. Moreover, it is self-evident that other things *do* exist. Science spins off from our physical senses, primarily vision; the entire scientific world is an enlargement by microscopes and telescopes of what we can see. But for all its importance, vision can't take in everything. No one has ever seen a thought. No one has ever seen a feeling. Yet our thoughts and feelings are where we primarily live our lives. It goes without saying that in the scientistic picture, we figure as robots in a meaningless world. Fortunately, common sense keeps breaking through to disrupt the scientistic picture, which is a far cry from common sense and at the opposite end of the spectrum from the Christian worldview. The Christian world-view is drenched with meaning throughout. Christians don't seek meaning. Along with other traditional people (traditional cultures are invariably religious), they eat it, drink it, swim in it, and become it. For the most part they don't even bother to ask if life is meaningful. They take for granted that it is.

So secularism, though it gained a foothold during the first great revolution described above, is now losing ground. With only the nontraditional portion of the world to work with, and with its fatal mistake—equating absence-of-evidence with evidence-of-absence—now exposed, modernity's (past-tense) scenario reads like this:

Beginning by ensconcing science as the royal road to knowl-edge (and conveniently overlooking the fact that humanity is fallen and in need of redemption from its sinful nature), modernity went on to predict that technology would ensure unending progress. Endless progress through the technological application of continuous scientific discovery—this is what modernity's scenario comes down to. And because it was founded on an illusion (the illusion that the scientific method is omnicompetent) it was inevitable that sooner or later it would bump into reality—in this case, history. And it now has, with a vengeance. The twentieth century, the most barbaric in history, makes the myth of progress read like a cruel joke: 160 million human beings slaughtered by their own kind; more people dying of starvation in a single decade than in all of history up to the twentieth century; AIDS epidemics in Africa and elsewhere; the widening gap between the rich and the poor; the environmental crisis; the threat of nuclear holocaust—the list goes on and on.

As for technology, it has given us a very peculiar form of paradise. The bloom started coming off the rose with Rachel Carlson's *Silent Spring,* which documented the deadly impact of pesticides. And, the charge that we are to be faithful stewards of the natural world having been ignored, the bloom has continued to fade from the technological rose. Better planes, better guns and gasses, better explosives—every improvement increases the sum of fear and hatred and escalates hysteria. Even the less destructive applications of technology aren't much more satisfactory, for what do they result in? The multiplication of possessable objects; the invention of new instruments of stimulation; the dissemination of new wants through propaganda aimed at equating possession with well-being and incessant stimulation with happiness. But incessant stimulation from without is a source of bondage, and so is preoccupation with possessions. Labor-saving devices have made us busier than ever, and we find ourselves trapped in a culture of haste that makes us a tired nation.

We have it from Archibald MacLeish that a world ends when its metaphor dies, and modernity's metaphor—endless progress through science-powered technology—is dead. It is only cultural lag—the backward pull of the outgrown good—that keeps us running on it.

Having been built on a shaky foundation, the institutions of contemporary culture are unstable. The institutions that rib society are principally science, technology, business, education, religion, media, art, and (presiding over all of them) government; and today none of these is serving us well. This could have been expected, for science cannot read into the picture even the minimal ethical principles, such as honesty, that institutions run on.

Let's take a look at the state of our major institutions:

- *Science* used to decide the next questions and then call for government's or business's support. Nowadays, it is government and business that set the agendas and then hire university scientists to do the work. The goal is patents. The sciences are increasingly engaged with technical rather than comprehensive approaches to things.

- *Technology* is disproportionately invested in, on the one hand, designing more effective instruments of death (and shields that might protect us from them) and, on the other hand, helping industries pour out new consumer goods that are not really needed.

- *Business* is reaching out for mergers, and with globalization, international conglomerates are increasingly exempt from governmental restraints. Competition for profits reigns, and with the "bottom line" running the show, the almighty dollar has become exactly that—almighty. The business paradigm, as it is now deployed, is widening the gap between the rich and the poor, both nationally and internationally.

- *Education*'s condition is enough to make one weep. In an interview shortly before his death, Isaac Asimov (one of the most successful science writers of all time) said that if he could have one wish for our society, it would be that it pour vastly more money into primary education, for the children in its custody are at their most malleable age when inputs make the most difference in their characters. His wish has not been granted. What's more, despite the fact that higher education has lost its sense of direction, it continues to call the tune, for it dispenses the credentials for public school teachers.

  I say that universities have lost their sense of direction because they have been diverted into becoming training institutes (for getting jobs and acquiring upward mobility) and grant-securing agencies. Alongside these two trends, the specialization that universities foster has cut the seamless fabric of knowledge into pieces called "academic disciplines" that work within departmental walls. Each of these disciplines has its own subject matter and feels free to develop its own methods for getting at it, perceiving no need to know what goes on outside its walls. Moreover, as disciplinary expertise deepens, disciplines divide into subdisciplines, leaving us with wheels within wheels, so to speak. This makes it impossible for universities to give their students perspective and understanding. The upshot is that—despite the fact that in a very real sense the university has become the established church of America, for a university degree is indispensable for staying in the swim of things—universities have become marginal to society.

- After biological needs are met, *religion* is the greatest resource people have, for it gives their lives meaning, motivation, and hope by holding out the promise of salvation if they live as they should. But today religion is hamstrung between liberals and conservatives who cancel each other out.

Conservative Christians, commonly tagged as fundamentalists, incline toward a biblical literalism that is unworkable because it ignores the contexts that give words their meaning—different contexts, different meanings—and they are in constant danger of slipping into disastrous political agendas.* Worse yet, they are untrue to Jesus. Jesus was invariably generous, whereas fundamentalists tend to be narrowly dogmatic and chauvinistic.

Liberal churches, for their part, are digging their own graves, for without a robust, emphatically theistic worldview to work within, they have nothing to offer their members except rallying cries to be good. We have it

---

* Dogmatic fundamentalism is usually associated with conservatives, but there are really two dogmatic fundamentalisms in America today. Dogmatic secular modernity came first and produced conservative religious fundamentalism as a reaction to it.

from Peter Berger that "if anything characterizes modernity it is the loss of the sense of transcendence—of a reality that exceeds and encompasses our everyday affairs." Universities incorporate that loss, and as clergy need to be educated, inevitably their university education rubs off on them and dilutes their confidence in transcendence. (The conservatives' grip on transcendence is no stronger.)

The chickens are coming home to roost; we are seeing the culmination of a two-century transformation of liberal theology into ethical philosophy, and piety into morality. Morality has become the foundation of liberal Christianity, rather than the reverse, and as a result the authority of religion has waned along with the mystery of the sacred. This capitulation to secularism is disastrous because, as Saul Bellow said, "it is hard to see how modern man can survive on what he now gets from his conscious life—now that there is a kind of veto against impermissible thoughts, the most impermissible being the notion that man might have a spiritual life he is not conscious of which reaches out for transcendence."

- The *media* have become big business, with mergers reducing the range of opinions, and audience ratings (which reveal what the public wants to hear) calling the tune. The *New York Review of Books,* which comes close to being the house organ for intellectuals in America, covers politics, history, science, biography, the arts, and virtually every other human domain of culture admirably, but it resolutely excepts religious faith, which it ignores as a relic of the outdated past and a tool for fanatics.

- *Art* used to aspire to transport us to higher planes of reality. (When Mickey Hart of the Grateful Dead band was asked why a member of the Dead was so fascinated with the multiphonic chanting of Tibetan lamas, he answered, "Because we are both in the transportation business.") But as science has no higher planes to transport us to, artists are left with only flatlands to deal with. Plotinus saw clearly that "he who beholds beauty becomes beautiful," but beauty has ceased to be a presiding word among artists. It has been largely replaced with impact through various channels—abstract art with its emphasis on form and shock value (the effort to startle us into seeing this world in a different way), satire, and self-expression, hopefully authentic. I may have overstated the case here. There are beautiful things being created today. Richard Lippold's chandelier that shimmers in the vaulted canopy over the altar of St. Mary's Cathedral in San Francisco—hundreds of free-standing rods of stainless steel, some gilded with silver, some with gold—is a truly great work of art. And some beautiful poetry is being written. But these are exceptions that prove the rule, as a visit to the Museum of Modern Art in New York City or a concert mounted by the New Music Society will attest.

  I once came upon a man in North India who had been a successful painter in California but who had moved with his family and for two years had been studying Tibetan Buddhism and the highly stylized, canonized art of icon painting. When I expressed surprise at his switch, he explained that in the States he'd tried to express himself on canvas, but that it hadn't taken him long to see that he had very little self to express. Back to the West, Hegel said of the art of his time: yes, people still write poetry and paint, but "however splendid the gods look in these modern works of art, and whatever dignity and perfection we might find in their images of God the Father and the Virgin Mary, it is of no use. We no longer bend our knees." That was two centuries ago.

- *Government,* which in a way presides over everything that goes on, requires from its people what it cannot itself provide—namely, meaning, motivation, and hope. And (as this quick review has indicated) because the institutions under government's wing are not providing these, business has taken over. As Gore Vidal points out, we really have only one political party in America today, the property party, and within it the highest bidders get their way. All of this is true despite the perception that as of this writing Washington is beholden to Christian fundamentalists. To the extent that this is true, it is Christianity hijacked for political purposes that is in the driver's seat.

One more component must be added to this list, even though it is more like an assumption than an institution:

- *Individualism.* Modernity induces us to believe that there is no right higher than the right to choose what one believes, wants, needs, or must possess. This gives us "the culture of narcissism" that Christopher Lasch described in his book by that title. We believe that our wills are sovereign because unpremised, free because spontaneous, and the highest endowment we have. The poet Rilke points out the consequence: "Let's be honest about it: We don't have a theater today any more than we have a God; for these community is needed." So steeped are we in rampant individualism that it may be difficult for us to realize that it is not universal. Many times when I have been in India and have been helped, the helper's response to my thanks has been not "You're welcome" but "It is my *dharma*, my duty." The concept of *dharma* attaches duty to truth and renders the response, "It is the duty God has imposed on me"—a far cry from what the helper might have been *inclined* to do.

At the same time, and at the opposite pole from individualism, melancholy in this late stage of secular modernity has become a collective mood. It used to afflict individuals who felt rejected and exiled from the significance of the cosmos. Today it is a cultural malady deriving from a world that has been drained of the meaning that religion guarantees and which casts doubt on all traditional sources—theological, metaphysical, historical. Add this mood and assumption to our society's shaky institutions and we are left with a society that is rudderless. Floundering.

It would be futile to try to suggest how these institutions might be shored up, for (as was indicated early on in this Introduction) they must first have a solid foundation to build on; and secular modernity, which is built on false premises, cannot provide it. The time has come to recognize that it was not something modernity *discovered* that set us on an unworkable course, but a mistake it made. Fortunately, mistakes can be corrected, and this second turning point in the history of spirit is witnessing that correction.

This book tries to contribute to that correction. On the eve of one of his decisive battles Napoleon Bonaparte is said to have exclaimed, "My center is not holding; my flanks are in disarray; I shall attack!" That decision is echoed in the football adage "The best defense is a good offense." From here on this book follows that strategy. It champions Christianity by telling the Christian story in a way that is more persuasive than secularism's attacks on it.

A historical anecdote (which happens to be a fascinating bit of Americana that should not be allowed to be forgotten) can launch us into the body of this book:

In the first half of the twentieth century the Tennessee Valley Authority was established to dam up a valley to generate electricity for that southern state. Officials went to the settlers in the designated valley to move them to other sites. The terms were satisfactory and people complied. With one exception—a holdout.

Typical Appalachian scene and dialect. The dialect is important because local English (which is being crowded out by the standard English that is now required of radio/television announcers) is a source of pleasure and exactitude.

An old man sitting on the narrow porch of his one-room cabin, smoking his corncob pipe, dog lying at his feet. (I'll skip the proverbial jug of moonshine—this is a true account, not a caricature.) The old man hears his visitors out and says, "I ain't movin'." Reasoning gets the negotiators nowhere, nor does upping the ante—more land, better house, etc. Same reply: "I ain't movin'."

When the bargaining recommences, the old man again hears them out and then says, "You don't get it, do you, boys? Come into my cabin. I want to show you something." Barest of amenities, but a fire is burning in the fireplace.

"See that fire, boys? My grandpappy started it, and when he died my pappy kept it going. If I move, that fire goes out. And now, boys, do you get it? I ain't movin'."

The negotiators left, and returned the next day with a bulldozer and a large flatbed truck. The bulldozer scooped the cabin onto the flatbed and, with the owner and his dog tagging along, deposited the cargo onto its new site.

The reader is probably already onto my point. This book tries to do its part to keep the Christian story from going out.

Kentucky isn't Tennessee but it abuts it, and as Wendell Berry is a farmer, a man of the soil (as were most of the people in the Tennessee Valley), we will let him make this same point less dramatically:

My grandson, who is four years old, is now following his father and me over some of the same countryside that I followed my father and grandfather over. When his time comes, my grandson will choose as he must, but so far all of us have been farmers. I know from my grandfather that when he was a child he too followed his father in

this way, hearing and seeing without consciously knowing that the most essential part of his education had
begun.

These preliminary sections of the book have been designed
to indicate the lay of the land—the historical context in which
this book is written. We are now ready to begin the book
proper.

—◆—

THE CHRISTIAN
WORLDVIEW

*The paradoxes of this world, ranging all the way from our
daily life to the paradoxes of quantum mechanics and relativity theory, are life and nature's way of repulsing a false philosophy, naturalism.*

The background of the Christian story is its two-tiered world,
which the Prologue to this book introduced by way of Plato's
Allegory of the Cave. In that allegory the dim outlines in the
cave contrast sharply with the lighted "outside world," which
serves as a metaphor for the "upper story" ("transcendence"
was Peter Berger's word for it) that all religious worldviews affirm. In East Asia Confucius made this point with definitive
succinctness: "Heaven and earth; only Heaven is Great." In
South Asia *samsara* is inferior to Nirvana, and in the Abrahamic family of religions Yahweh/God/Allah created the universe. Without an upper story, the ultimacy of an Infinite
God-by-whatsoever-name makes no sense, any more than do
Jesus's true nature, the redemption of a fallen humanity,
prayer, salvaton, etc. And come to think of it, science doesn't

make sense either. Frontier scientists are always working on the rim of the infinite, for beyond the edge of today's universe lies the infinite unknown we will step into tomorrow. And the same holds when we peer into the seemingly infinite depths of the atom. This part of the book—Part One—blueprints the world's upper story by way of pinpointing its fixed points, numbered in the text below, in the conviction that if they are kept clearly in mind the Christian story will come through to us more sharply.

Before beginning to list the points, we should take note of the background within which they are positioned. *The Christian world is objective,* in the sense that it was here before we were and that it is our business to understand it. "Honor the object, not the subject," Czeslaw Milosz admonished, and Christianity does that.

This was taken for granted until modern philosophy introduced idealism as the opposite of realism. Science remains realistic because it can demonstrate what the world is like without us, but for the rest, modernity assumes that we must begin with how the world *appears* to us and extrapolate from there. William Blake was quick to notice the mistake here: once you begin with a self/world divide (as animals and traditional peoples do not), there is no way Humpty Dumpty can be put back together again. As he wrote,

The dim window of our soul
Distorts the heavens from pole to pole
And leads us to believe the lie
That we see with, not thro', the eye.

That said, we can proceed to enumerate the fixed points of the Christian world—or rather, the Christian worldview, for it includes smaller worlds that nest within it like Chinese boxes, as the closing stanza of the hymn "Rock of Ages" attests:

While I breathe this fleeting breath,
When I close my eyes at death,
When I rise to worlds unknown,
and behold thee on thy throne;
Rock of Ages, cleft for me,
let me hide myself in thee.

1. *The Christian world is Infinite,* for if you stop with finitude you face a door with only one side, an absurdity. The Infinite has *doorways,* but not *doors.*

2. *The Infinite includes the finite* or we would be left with infinite-plus-finite and the Infinite would not be what it claims to be. The natural image to depict the Infinite's inclusiveness is a circle, an all-including circle that encompasses our finite universe and out of which it is impossible to fall. "In Him we live and move and have our being," Paul tells us, and Augustine added, "God is a circle whose center is everywhere and whose circumference is nowhere."

The point here is God's pervasiveness, and it needs to be experienced, not just affirmed. Jonathan Edwards described how God's pervasiveness was brought home to him in the course of a long, contemplative walk in his father's pasture, and how that walk showed him that God's pervasiveness

THE SOUL OF CHRISTIANITY

required that God's majesty include, not exclude, meekness as well. It is an important point, so I will quote him in full:

> My sense of Divine things gradually increased and became more and more lively and had more sweetness. The appearance of everything was altered; there seemed to be as it were a calm, sweet cast or appearance of Divine Glory in almost everything. God's excellence, His wisdom, His purity and love, seemed to appear in everything: in the sun, moon, and stars; in the clouds and blue sky; in the grass, flowers, trees; in the water and all nature, which used greatly to fix my mind. I often used to sit and view the moon for a long time, and so in the day time spent much time in viewing the clouds and sky to behold the sweet glory of God in these things, in the meantime singing forth with a low voice my contemplations of the Creator and Redeemer. And scarce anything among all the works of nature were so sweet to me as thunder and lightning: formerly nothing had been so terrible to me. I used to be a person uncommonly terrified with thunder, and it used to strike me with terror when I saw a thunderstorm rising. But now on the contrary it rejoiced me. I felt God at the first appearance of a thunderstorm and used to take the opportunity at such times to fix myself to view the clouds and see the lightning's play and hear the majesty and awful voice of God's thunder, which led me to sweet contemplations of my great and glorious God; and while I viewed I used to spend my time singing or chanting for my meditations, speaking my thoughts in soliloquies—speaking with a singing voice.

3. The contents of the finite world are hierarchically ordered. Arthur Lovejoy titled his important study in the history of philosophy *The Great Chain of Being* and argued that its underlying idea had been accepted by most educated people throughout the world until modernity mistakenly abandoned it in the late eighteenth century. *The Great Chain of Being* presents the idea of a universe composed of an infinite number of links ranging in hierarchical order from the meagerest kind of existence through every possible grade up to the boundless Infinite. The ascent may be a smooth continuum, but for practical purposes it helps to divide it into categories—steps on a ladder, so to speak. Aristotle's categories of mineral, vegetable, animal, and rational remain useful but stop too soon. Human beings are only midway up the chain. Above them are heavenly choirs of angels, symbolized by Jacob's dream of angels ascending and descending on a ladder that reached from earth to heaven. In the third century, Origen inverted the ladder to point out that causation is from the top downward: "All things started from one beginning," he said,

> but were distributed throughout the different ranks of existence in accordance with their merit; for in them goodness does not rest essentially, as it does in God and His Christ and in the Holy Spirit. For only in this Trinity, which is the source of all things, does goodness reside essentially. Others possess it as an accident, liable to be lost, and only then do they live in blessedness when they participate in holiness and wisdom and in the Divine nature itself.

4. *Causation is from the top down, from the Infinite down through the descending degrees of reality.* This brings us to another reason why (as was suggested in the Introduction) the West may now be more open to hearing the Christian story: emerging evidence is forcing scientists to reconsider their "bottom-up" theory of causation, which has challenged the Christian position. This bears looking into.

Since science is empirical, everything in it spins off from our physical senses. The fact that those senses connect only with physical objects and that the entire house of science is founded on our physical senses led scientists to assume that matter is the fundamental stuff of the universe. Their familiar scenario begins with the Big Bang, from which issued the smallest conceivable entities—quarks, strings, what have you—that grouped themselves into progressively more complex entities until in the latest nanosecond of cosmic time life and consciousness emerged. It's upward causation all the way.

What is causing scientists to reconsider that scenario is their dawning realization that it contains no explanation for *why* complexity increases. To say that it rides the Big Bang's momentum is no good, for no one knows what powered the Big Bang in the first place. And to say that the complex forms *emerged* fares no better, for emergence is a descriptive, not an explanatory, concept. (Time out to reflect on this for a moment and let this regularly overlooked point sink in.)

All this is leading scientists to think that the foundational feature of the universe is not matter but information. This changes the job of science, which scientists have assumed is to identify underlying structures that have to obey certain equations no matter what. Now, however, the world is seen as a hierarchy of nested systems—holons—that convey information, and the job of physical theory is to extract as much information from these systems as possible. This frees science from the reductionistic project of forcing nature into its procrustean, empirical bed and turns scientists into inquirers who ask nature questions, obtaining answers and always remaining open to the possibility that nature has deeper levels of information to divulge. Nothing of substance in mechanistic science is lost. The thing that does give way is the idea that physics is a bottom-up affair in which knowledge of a system's parts determines knowledge of the system as a whole. In the informational approach the whole is invariably greater than the sum of its parts, which the Christian worldview asserts in its top-down causation.

5. *In descending to finitude, the singularity of the Infinite splays into multiplicity*—the One becomes the many. The parts of the many are virtues, for they retain in lesser degree the signature of the One's perfection. The foundational virtue is existence, for to be more than figments of the imagination, virtues must exist. The Scholastic dictum put it like this: *Esse qua esse bonum est,* "Being as being is good." It is good simply to exist—a real loaf of bread is better than an imagined one. As for what the virtues other than existence are, India begins the list with *sat, chit,* and *ananda* (being, consciousness, and bliss). The West's ternary is the good, the true, and the beautiful, and these beginnings open out into creativity, compassion, and love until we arrive at Islam's Ninety-nine Beautiful Names of God, which include the Holy, the Forgiver, the Gentle, the Incomparable, the Glorious, and their likes. Above these lies the

hundredth name, which—symbolically absent from the Islamic rosary—is unutterable.

6. As we look upward from our position on the causal chain, we find that *as the virtues ascend the causal ladder, they expand* in the way one's chest does when one takes a deep breath and inhales air, which in this example stands for God. *As virtues expand they begin to overlap; their distinctions fade and they begin to merge.* This requires that the images of ladder and chain be replaced with that of a pyramid. Flannery O'Connor titled one of her books *Everything That Rises Must Converge,* and this is so. (Teilhard de Chardin says the same. The longitudinal lines on our planet do this as they converge at the north and south poles.) At the top of the pyramid, God knows lovingly and loves knowingly, and so on, until in God's infinity differences (which betoken separation) disappear completely in the divine "simplicity," a technical term that can be likened to a mathematical point that has no extension. (There is nothing simple about a "simplicity" that includes everything. We might speak of distinctions without differences, but no amount of verbal legerdemain of this sort can do anything more than paper over the profound paradoxes we run into when we try to understand God with our finite minds.) To name that mathematical point, any virtue will serve as long as the word is capitalized, whereupon the words become synonyms. God is the conventional English name for the Infinite, but Good, True, Real, Almighty, One, etc., are equally accurate.

7. To go back to the mathematical point, when power and goodness (and the other virtues) converge at the top of the

pyramid, the Christian worldview's most staggering claim comes to view: *absolute perfection reigns.*

- "Snow flakes falling, flake by flake, / Each flake falls/in its own proper place" (Zen haiku).

- "Despite the fact that the world is in about the worst possible shape imaginable, at the eye of the cyclone all is well" (Hegel).

- "I was shown in a vision that all things that are done are well done, so there is no need for mercy or grace, for already in themselves nothing is amiss" (Julian of Norwich).

This brings us face-to-face with the problem of evil. Evil is the Rock of Gibraltar that every rational philosophy runs into and is smashed to splinters by. To come to terms with it, we must look at it from a different angle, a higher religious angle. From that angle the story reads like this:

God endowed human beings with intelligence and freedom, without which they would be mere puppets. Freedom brings with it the capacity to make mistakes. God did not force human beings to sin—that would have been to retract the freedom he had given them—but somewhere along the line a mistake was made, and it entered into the human bloodstream (or gene pool as we would now say), thereby saddling humanity with original sin— "original" not in the temporal meaning of that word, but in the sense of being archetypally universal, a template from which variations arise. In the biblical, metaphorical narrative Adam and Eve were created sinless but made the mistake of eating forbidden fruit, and this act expelled them from paradise, outside of which their descendants continue to live. We are mixed bags, capable of great nobility and horrendous evil. Our besetting sin is to put ourselves ahead of others; egotism or self-centeredness is built into us. We cannot get rid of that handicap, but we can and must work at restraining it.

8. The "great chain of being" with its links of increasing worth needs to be extended by the classical formula "As above, so below." In other words, *everything that is outside us is also inside us:* "The kingdom of God is within you." We intersect and inhabit all the echelons of the chain of being, as Sir Thomas Browne realized and recorded in his seventeenth-century *Religio Medici:* "Man is a multiple amphibian, disposed to live, not only like other creatures in diverse elements, but in divided and distinguishable worlds." To understand these worlds requires that we introduce a short discussion on the symbolism of space.

Four sentences from C. E. Rolt's introduction to *Dionysius the Areopagite: On the Divine Names and the Mystical Theology* can get us started. "Spatial metaphors are always dangerous though unavoidable in Theology," he writes. "In space, if A is touching B then B must be touching A. In the spiritual world this is not so. God is near me (or rather in me), and yet I may be far from God because I may be far from my own true self." We can apply this to the matter at hand as follows:

Envisioned externally, as residing outside and apart from us, the Good dons metaphors of height: gods always dwell on mountaintops, and angels sing on high. When we reverse our gaze and look inward, the spatial imagery does a flip-over and turns upside down. Within us the best lies deepest inside us: it is basic, fundamental, the ground of our being. That which outside ourselves we seek in the highest heavens, inwardly we seek in the depths of our souls. The following diagram presents our amphibious nature, the multiple worlds we inhabit, visually.

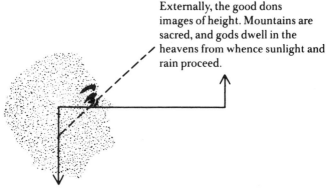

Externally, the good dons images of height. Mountains are sacred, and gods dwell in the heavens from whence sunlight and rain proceed.

Internally, the good dons images of depth. We sense it as centered, like the heart and other vital organs, within a protective sheath of bone and sinew.

The complete picture shows the ineffable, unutterable, *apophatic Godhead* at the top, descending through the personal, describable, *kataphatic God,* on down to *angels* and from there to the *physical universe.* Regarding ourselves, *mind* is more important than *body,* our souls (which Aristotle said animate our mind-filled bodies) are more important than either of the foregoing, and Spirit is the breath of God—the *imago Dei* which is the foundation of our being.

9. *We cannot know the Infinite.* Because we are in it, intimations of it will seep into us occasionally, but more than this we cannot manage on our own. If we are to know it confidently, the Infinite must take the initiative and show itself to us. If there is to be a love affair between the Infinite and the finite, the Infinite must do the wooing. Hence Revelation, *re-velum,* unveiling, the pulling back of the curtain that hides the Infinite from the finite, God from the world.

10. *Revelation is multiple in both scope and degree;* it has both horizontal breadth and vertical depth. "The Gospel combines in itself both width and straitness" (Dionysius the Areopagite). I begin with its breadth:

Civilizations differ, the better to flesh out the full scope of the human potential which no single civilization can circumscribe. "Had Allah willed He could have made you one community," we read in the Koran, "but He hath made you as you are. So vie one with another in good works. Unto Allah you will all return, and He will then inform you of that wherein you differ" (V:48). The phrase "unto Allah you will all return" is ambiguous. Here it indicates that all revelations are paths to salvation; as peoples understand only their own language, "never did We send any messenger save with the language of his people, that he might make the message clear to them" (XIV:14). The single Revelation expresses itself in different idioms—which is to say, in different lowercase revelations, all of which contain truth sufficient unto salvation. Whether all people are saved will be dealt with later.

Being earlier, Christianity was more isolated than Islam, so the doctrine of universal salvation was less needed in Christianity while that faith was housed within its own cocoon. Origen's affirmation of it in the third century was called into question at the Fifth Ecumenical Council three centuries later, but even so, St. Vincent of Lérins—whose canon concerning "what has been believed everywhere, always, and by all" is the very definition of orthodoxy—said that he would rather be wrong with Origen than right with the world. Now, however, in our globalized, multicultural world, the belief in universal salvation has become important, and obstacles to it must be dealt with.

The chief of these is the claim to superiority, which appears in every religion. In Christianity its most emphatic instance is in Peter's uncompromising assertion to rulers and elders that "there is salvation in no one else [save Jesus], for there is no other name under heaven given among men whereby we must be saved" (Acts 4:12). And to cite only one instance from another tradition, legend has it that the Buddha at his birth declared, "I alone am the most honored in heaven and on earth"; and again, "As the footprints of all animals are contained in the footprint of the elephant, so are all *dharmas* [religions] contained in the teaching of the Enlightened One." Claims like these can be tempered to some extent by recognizing that the heavens and earth the speakers had in mind were provincial—those that they and their hearers were involved with—but the deeper point is this: revelations are for the civilizations they create, and within each the truths revealed *are* absolute and can brook no rivals. There is no dissembling here: when a man says that his wife means the world to him, he is not claiming that she should mean the world to other men. Moreover, underlying the "relative absolute" in his assertion, there is an absolute Absolute: he *does* believe that all men should feel for their wives the *love* that he feels for his wife. In our multicultural age Christians are coming to understand this point. Only a minority of Christians (for the most part evangelical Protestants of a fundamentalistic bent, conservative Catholics, and Orthodox who take the teaching "outside the church there is no salvation" parochially) now claim that all non-Christians will go to hell. Furthermore, nonexclusivism has been affirmed throughout Christian history, though not by the majority. Four examples are worth mentioning:

- From the seventh to the twelfth century, a splendid, thriving interfaith civilization flourished in medieval Spain. Christianity, Islam, and Judaism not only tolerated but actively engaged one another. They drew on one another's artistic and spiritual resources while maintaining the integrity of their own traditions.

- In the sixteenth century a Franciscan friar, Geronimo de Mendieta, who went to New Spain (Mexico) as a missionary, after living with the Indians for a time came to regard them as a *genus angelicum,* an isolated fragment of the human race that had retained the primordial innocence, simplicity, and purity that Adam and Eve had known in the Garden of Eden. A nude Indian woman, he said, was purer than a European lady finely attired. He claimed that the American Indians practiced, almost intuitively, all of the spiritual virtues taught by Jesus in the Sermon on the Mount.

- A twentieth-century example is the French Benedictine monk Dom Henri Le Saux, who chose India as his mission field. On encountering the Hindu saint Ramana Maharshi, he became convinced that Advaita Vedanta and Christian doctrine are but two forms of an identical Truth, and assumed the name Abhishiktananda, Bliss of the Anointed One. He lived for the rest of his life in a hermitage in the Himalayas near the source of the Ganges. Father Bede Griffiths followed him, likening religions to the fingers of a single hand, separate but working together.

- A more recent example is Wilfred Cantwell Smith, who as a missionary to Lahore, Pakistan, became fluent in Arabic. When the troubles over the partition of Pakistan from India necessitated his return to North America, he became a distinguished professor of Islamic studies. Although he himself remained a committed Christian, he required his advanced students at McGill University to observe the four mandatory "pillars of Islam": recite the creed—"There is no God but God, and Muhammad is his prophet" (students could change Muhammad to a prophet of their own choosing if they wished); pray five times a day at the stipulated times while facing Mecca; give alms to the poor; and fast from dawn to sunset if the course they were taking fell during the month of Ramadan. (The fifth pillar is not mandatory in Islam. Only those who can afford to undertake a pilgrimage to Mecca and can do so without inordinate inconvenience are required to observe the *hajj,* and in any case non-Muslims would not be admitted to Mecca.)

These examples betoken a new mood in Christendom, a more conscious, general recognition that though for Christians God is *defined by* Jesus, he is not *confined to* Jesus.

I turn now to Revelation's degrees. Its paradigmatic instances are those in which God burst into human consciousness with a force that creates civilizations. To wit:

- Moses on Mount Sinai. Thunder cracks the mountaintop. Thick smoke in a fiery plume darkens the sky. Flashes of lightning illuminate the dense cloud cover as the deafening wail of the ram's horn blares long and urgent shrieks into the night. Sharp trumpet blasts pierce the thunderbolts and shake the mountain. The ground where the Hebrews stand undulates with violent waves as a sea ripped by hurricane. The whole top of the mountain is a furnace vomiting black smoke as the devouring firestorm descends on the peaks. Then, with a series of spasms, the earth settles and the mountain grows quiet; blasts of the ram's horn, long, deafening, slowly fade. The sky clears and Moses descends from the mountain with the words he heard at its top: "I am YHVH. I am your God." But the Israelites cannot see Moses, for he shines like a red-hot iron removed from the flame.

- Jesus emerges from the waters of the Jordan after his baptism, sees the heavens open and the Spirit descending upon him like a dove, and hears a voice saying, "Thou art my beloved Son; with thee I am well pleased."

- Saul, knocked off his horse and struck blind on the Damascus road, hears a voice saying, "Saul, Saul, why do you persecute me?" He then becomes Paul, and the Christian church gains a foothold in history.

Theophanies of this magnitude endow their recipients with a charisma that rubs off onto their disciples, and this is Revelation's first extension. The records of what came through Moses, Jesus, and Paul, the Gospels and Acts, lack the immediacy of face-to-face contacts and so are a step further removed from the source, and theological reflections yet another step. All are the same Revelation, fading gradually as the distance from the source increases.

11. *Reports have to be interpreted—hence the science of exegesis.* This science, which became codified as early as the third century with Origen, mounts through four steps of ascending importance: literal, ethical, allegorical, and anagogic. *Literal:* What does the text explicitly assert? That Jesus was crucified, for example. *Ethical:* What does the text tell us we should and should not do? *Allegorical:* What are the meanings that Jesus's parables, for example, convey? And finally, *anagogic:* What inspiration can we draw from the text? I want to insert a personal word on the last and most important of these four questions we should put to texts.

Joseph Campbell, a longstanding friend of mine, did more than anyone else in the twentieth century to counter our secular culture's simplistic equation of myth with superstition— "the myth of the superrace" is the flag-waving example.

Reinhold Niebuhr had already noted that "myth is not history, it is truer than history," and my approving allusion to his insight in my term paper for a graduate seminar on logical positivism came close to earning me the only failing grade I would ever receive. Myth is "truer than history," Niebuhr explained, because it refers to Transcendence, which (as the next section of this book will spell out in detail) cannot be accurately described in human language. It has to be circled and approached obliquely:

> Tell the truth but tell it slant,
> Success in circuit lies;
> Too bright for mind's infirm intent,
> Is truth's sublime surmise.
> Like lightning to the children eased,
> Through revelation kind;
> The truth must dazzle gradually,
> Or every man be blind.
>
> Emily Dickinson

Coming back to Joseph Campbell, early on we agreed to divide mythology's turf between us: he would defend its power and I its truth. (Joe was too bruised by his Irish Catholic upbringing to be a believer.) Now to the point of this reminiscence. Joe's popular television series with Bill Moyers, *The Power of Myth*, gave his generation a slogan to live by: "Follow your bliss." It's not bad, but writing this book has led me to conclude that "Follow your aspiration or inspiration" is better. Bliss comes in many shapes and sizes, not all of which are noble—cocaine, for example—whereas the words "inspire" and "inspiration" point us upward and are themselves inspiring. The word "spirit" derives from "breath." To breathe is to inhale spirit—Christians turn this into the Holy Spirit—and to aspire is to ride spirit to higher realms. (Gregory of Nyssa, one of the greatest of the church fathers, is best known for his paradoxical idea—"reaching forward" is the literal translation of his Greek—that perfection consists in an endless attempt to reach perfection.)

To complete this meditation on the anagogic, climactic way to interpret and learn from a text, I can report that though I always enjoy writing, writing about religion gives me the greatest pleasure, because at religion's best (the part I dwell on), it inspires me. This makes writing about it enjoyable, and more. It brings the kind of fulfillment Aristotle called *flourishing* and makes my mornings a holy time—by extension, a time of prayer.

12. It follows from the above that *exegesis that stops with the literal meaning of a text*—the lowest of the four steps on the ladder—*cannot do that text full justice.* Classical Christianity took it for granted that literalism could not do the full job, which is why "Jesus spoke to them in parables." Paul overreacted to his heritage when he contrasted the Old Covenant's "letter that kills" with the New Covenant's "Spirit that gives life," but his underlying point that the Spirit exceeds the letter is correct. Origen, in speaking of Ezekiel's vision, wrote, "I do not imagine that the visible heavens were opened, or its physical form divided"; and he went on to add, "Perhaps the intelligent reader of the gospel ought give a similar interpretation in respect of the Savior's vision following his

baptism, even if this opinion may cause offense to the simple minded who in their extreme naiveté move the world and rend the vast, solid mass of the entire heaven." A century later St. Augustine dismissed truncated exegesis in a short treatise titled *The Literal Meaning of Genesis*. The twentieth century, however, witnessed the emergence of fundamentalism, and the literalism that perspective fixes on has generated so much confusion that it justifies an excursus to indicate its mistake.

A cautionary note must be entered before proceeding. Languages are geared to the worldviews that monitor them, and the sea change from the traditional to the scientistic worldview has profoundly affected the way our language works. The limitations of literalism were (as we have seen) recognized early on, but traditionally the literal meanings of scripture had a wider range of accuracy and effectiveness (that is, reached higher on the ladder of meaning) then than they do now: the virgin birth and empty tomb could be accepted at face value with no questions asked. And to the extent that we can do that today we are fortunate, for it shows that we haven't fallen into modernity's trap and made the everyday world our language's primary referent. But not many people today are this fortunate, and the following paragraphs are intended to help them cope with the difficulty that they have taking claims such as the two just cited—the virgin birth and the empty tomb—literally.

Science has shown us that there are three domains of size— the *microworld* of quantum mechanics, where distance is measured in *picometers;* the *macroworld* that we inhabit, where distance is measured in inches, feet, and miles; and the *megaworld* of the astronomers and relativity theory, where size is measured in light-years. Neither of the two worlds that flank ours can be consistently described in ordinary language: try to do so and you run into the contradictions that plague cartographers when they try to portray our three-dimensional planet on the two-dimensional pages of geography books—Greenland always balloons absurdly. Scientists can, however, describe the micro- and megaworlds consistently in their technical language, which is mathematics with its equations. Now, God is at least as different from our human world as are the micro- and megaworlds, because he includes them—remember, the Infinite is that out of which you cannot fall. It follows from this that if we stick to the Bible's literal assertions, we find ourselves in a tangle of contradictions analogous to those that scientists encounter when they try to draw verbal pictures of their subjects. We can almost hear the despair in Robert Oppenheimer's voice when he tells us, "If we ask whether the electron's position changes with time we must say 'No'; if we ask whether the position of the electron remains the same, we must say 'No'; if we ask whether the electron is at rest, we must say 'No'; if we ask whether it is in motion, we must say 'No'." ("If it is not paradoxical, it isn't true," says Shunryu Suzuki.) And we too are driven to despair if we stay with the contradictions that the Bible's actual words confront us with, as the following assemblage of spliced-together passages indicates:

> We become ourselves by dying to ourselves. We gain only what we give up, and if we give up everything we gain everything. We cannot find ourselves within ourselves, but only in others; yet at the same time, before we can go out to others we must first find ourselves. We must forget ourselves in order to become truly conscious

THE SOUL OF CHRISTIANITY

of who we are. The best way to love ourselves is to love others; yet we cannot love others unless we love ourselves, since it is written, "Thou shalt love thy neighbor as thyself." But if we love ourselves in the wrong way, we become incapable of loving anybody else. And indeed when we love ourselves wrongly we hate ourselves, and if we hate ourselves we cannot help hating others. Yet there is a sense in which we must hate others and leave them in order to find God: Jesus said, "If any man come to me, and hate not his father, and mother ... yea, and his own life also, he cannot be my disciple."

As for this "finding" of God, we cannot even look for him unless we have already found him, and we cannot find him unless he has first found us. We cannot begin to seek him without a special gift of his grace, yet if we wait for grace to move us before beginning to seek him, we will probably never begin.

To resume the argument, which has the force of a syllogism: as long as we remain on the human plane, the only way of dealing with these paradoxes is to reach out and embrace both extremes of the contradictions. (Laughter, it has been said, is where the opposites of life come together.) Only from a higher step on the ladder, one that gives us a wider view, can we see that these contradictions are actually paradoxes—which is to say, *seeming* contradictions that can be resolved in a multileveled view of things. To cite a simple example, if we see a locomotive going away and some time later returning to us on the same tracks, but facing now in the opposite direction, the matter (if left there) would be illogical. But if we were to climb a hill and see that around the bend there was a turnstile, there would be no problem. Theologically, the situation is the same: only from a higher plane of reality can the paradoxes of our daily live be resolved.

But to access that higher plane requires a technical language comparable to science's technical language, which as we have seen is mathematics. Religion's technical language is symbolism, the science of the relations between the multiple levels of reality.

More fully, religion's technical language is sacred art in its inclusive sense, which covers music, paintings (such as icons), as well as poetry, myths, metaphors, parables, figures of speech, and stories. (Plato calls stories that deflect our attention upward "likely tales" to indicate that it is the nonliteral connotations of their words that are important.) Prose is useful as a medium of exchange, which, like money, ordinarily serves us well, but in times of crisis we look for bread, in this context the bread of life, which transports us to a higher plane of reality.

My neighbors, how can I tell you about Essence when you do not even understand stories. If you only knew how great the sweetness, the expanse, and the strength are when one reaches the bottom of all the stories— there where the stories begin and where they end; there, where the tongue is silent and where everything is told at once. How boring all the lengthy and tedious stories of creatures then become! Truly, they become just as boring as it is for one who is accustomed to seeing lightning to hear stories about lightning.

St. Nicolai Velimirovich

THE SOUL OF CHRISTIANITY

The upshot of all this is that it is not possible to read scripture seriously if we stay within the stifling confines of literalism. Two anecdotes can help to drive that point home, so I will conclude the important point of this excursus—important because it gives the lie to troublemaking literalism—with these anecdotes:

I once had the opportunity to ask Saul Bellow whether an incident in one of his novels really happened. In the dead of a cold, windy night in Chicago's Windy City, an underworld "friend," to establish his dominance over Bellow, walked him out to the end of the horizontal arm of a huge sky-hook derrick, took three crisp one hundred dollar bills from his coat pocket, folded them into airplanes, and launched them out over the rooftops of Chicago. Bellow described the incident with such vividness that it made me think it had actually happened. Did it, I wanted to know? "Something like that," was all he said. It seems flippant to say that "something like" the virgin birth and the empty tomb happened, but we must remember that the alternative to that wording is to stay trapped in literalism. There is a charming story of a New Testament scholar who couldn't wait to get to heaven so he could ask St. Paul if he did write the Letter to the Ephesians, as most New Testament scholars assume. When he got his chance, Paul thought for a moment, stroked his beard, and said, "Yes, I think I did," which is as much as to say, Who cares?

My second anecdote is from the Native Americans. I heard one of them try to throw a bridge to the white man's outlook by describing a cure that a medicine man had accomplished. There was a very sick man in the tribe, and the medicine man was summoned to effect the cure. A nearby anthropologist got word of the happening and turned up to watch the affair. The cure was accomplished quite quickly, and the anthropologist wanted to know how it had been done. The medicine man said that his incantation and gestures had rid the patient of the ants that were swarming all over the patient's body, inside and out. When the anthropologist protested that he hadn't seen any ants, the medicine man stared at him in incomprehension for quite a while, as if trying to figure out what he might say that would get through to this stranger. Finally he gave up and blurted out, "Not ants, *Ants!*" and walked off. In the terms I am using, what he said was, Not everyday ants, but metaphysical Ants.

C. S Lewis said something that can serve as a useful commentary on these anecdotes. We are screened from reality by two facades, he pointed out: the room I see myself in, and the "I" that perceives it. But the moment I see these as mere facades, they become conductors. A lie is a delusion only if it is accepted at face value. Consider this hypothetical example:

Say I hired a gardener and went off for the day. When he showed up the next day and I asked him how many hours he had worked, he answered three, and I paid him accordingly. But I had left at ten that morning, and my wife, who had come home for the day at noon, later told me she hadn't seen hide nor hair of a workman. He had lied, but because I had believed him I had not taken his assertion as a lie; I had accepted it as true. Only when I put two and two together and recognized that he had lied did I see his assertion for what it truly was, a lie. Applying this to the anecdote about ants, to recognize that it is untrue (a lie) to think that ants are of one species only, mundane ants, is useful, for it implies that there is a higher level of truth in which ants assume their true, metaphysical character, as Ants.

Lewis makes this point in a discussion of prayer. "The moment of true prayer arrives," he says,

> when I recall that the "real world" and the "real self" are very far from being rock bottom realities. I cannot, in the flesh, leave the stage, either to go behind the scenes or to take my seat in the pit; but I can remember that these regions exist. And I can remember that my apparent self—the clown, or hero, or supernumerary—under his grease paint is a real person with an off stage life. The dramatic person could not tread the stage unless he concealed a real person: unless the real and unknown "I" existed. I would not even make mistakes about the imagined me. And in prayer this real "I" struggles to speak for itself and to address not the other actors, but what shall I call him? The Author, for he invented us all? The Producer, for he controls all? Or the Audience, for He watches, and will judge, the performance?

This is subtle but profound and well worth pondering, so I will let it stand.

13. Continuing with the "ribs" of Christianity's worldview, *there are two distinct and complementary ways of knowing, rational and intuitive.* "The intuitive mind is a sacred gift and the rational mind is its faithful servant," Einstein told us. The life and career of Blaise Pascal throw the two into exceptionally sharp relief. When he exclaimed, in what was to become his famous apho-

rism, "The heart has its reasons the mind knows not of," the "mind" he was thinking of was his scientific mind through which he achieved fame for his theory of probability in mathematics and his work on hydrodynamics in physics; and "heart" was his word for the organ through which burst the epiphany that turned his concern from science to religion: "FIRE. God of Abraham ... Isaac ... Jacob. Not the philosophers and the learned. . . . Tears of Joy. . . . My God . . . let me not be separated from thee for ever." But that he never intended to dismiss philosophy and learning in total is amply evidenced by his eighteen closely reasoned *Lettres Provençales* ("Provincial Letters"), in which he examined the fundamental problems of human existence, and by the entries in his notebook, titled *Pensées* ("Thoughts"), in which he spelled out his conviction that the true function of reason is to attain the truth or supreme good.

All the wisdom traditions spell this out carefully. In the West, intellect (*intellectus, gnosis, sapientia*) is not reason (*ratio*). In Sanskrit, *buddhi* is not *manas*. In Islam *ma'rifah*, situated in the heart, is not *aql*, situated in the brain. In Hinduism, the knowledge that effects union with God is not discursive; it has the immediacy of direct vision, of sight. In Greece, *theoria* referred to the kind of knowledge that one derived from watching the great Greek dramas. Our word "theater," which derives from it, is closer to its meaning than our word "theory," which has degenerated from *theoria* in much the way "belief" has degenerated from *more* than knowledge ("conviction and the determination to act on it") to something *less* than knowledge: "He believed that the world was flat" (the Oxford English Dictionary's example). Put poetically, in the words of Edna St. Vincent Millay, "The world stands out on either side / No wider than the heart is wide. /

The soul can split the sky in two, / and let the light of God shine through." And mystically, as in John of Ruysbroeck's description of the summit of the intellect's working:

> In the simple and abysmal tasting of all good and of eternal life we are swallowed up above reason and without reason are in the deep quiet of the Godhead which is never moved. That this is true we can know only by our own feeling and in no other way. For how this is, or where, or what, neither reason nor practice can come to know; and therefore our ensuing exercise always remains wayless, that is, without manner. For that abysmal good which we taste and possess, reason can neither grasp nor understand; neither can we enter into it by ourselves or by means of our exercises.

Back to the everyday world: we all have hunches; some pay off, others don't. Hunches are rudimentary forms of intuitive knowing. Every scientific discovery begins with hunches. Reason and experiments must immediately enter to test the hunches, and here too we encounter the underlying truth of this section: that in human thought, reason and intuition must work together.

14. Walnuts have shells that house kernels, and *religions likewise have outsides and insides*: they have *outer, exoteric forms that house inner, esoteric cores.* People differ on which of these stands out more clearly for them. For esoterics God is in focal view, whereas for exoterics his created world is focal and God must be inferred from it. It follows that for exoterics this

world is concrete and the celestial world is abstract, whereas for esoterics it is the other way around. I once heard an eminent philosopher of religion say that when he was asked for proofs of God's existence he didn't know where to begin, because God's existence seemed to him more apparent than anything he could prove his existence *from*.

To elaborate on this difference, it will help to recall the sixth point in this outline of the Christian worldview that we are working on. For esoterics, only God at the tip of the pyramid of virtues is completely real, and because he occupies no space he is formless. Esoterics are comfortable with this, but exoteric minds require forms—diagrams, words, propositions—to work with. C. S. Lewis provides us with a good example of an exoteric Christian. He tells us that when he was a child his parents pounded into him that he should not ascribe a form to God, for God is unlimited and beyond all forms. Lewis tells us that he tried and tried to imagine a formless God, but the closest he could come was an endless sea of gray tapioca. Precisely! It follows that exoterics need to think of God in personal terms, whereas esoterics (while sometimes clothing God in human attributes) recognize the danger of anthropomorphism—making God too human—and therefore complement their "personal" God with what Lewis's parents were getting at. We require that God be both like and unlike us—like us so we can connect with him, and different from us because we cannot worship our own kind. Absolute imminence and absolute transcendence in absolute tension is what gives maximal tonus to our spiritual lives.

In his magisterial classic *The Divine Names*, Dionysius the Areopagite pushed the transcendent pole as far as words can carry us:

Guide us to that topmost height of mystic lore ["mystic" is a passable synonym for "esoteric"] which surpasses light and more than surpasses knowledge, where the simple, absolute unchangeable mysteries of heavenly Truth lie hidden in the dazzling obscurity of the secret Silence, outshining all brilliance with the intensity of their darkness, and surcharging our blinded intellects with the utterly impalpable and invisible fairness of glories which exceed all beauty.

But almost every other passage of such mystical soaring in *The Divine Names* is followed by a verse of the Bible that, like a kite string, ties it to things we can readily understand.

One more difference between esoterics and exoterics should be mentioned. Esoterics can understand exoterics and recognize the need for them, but the reverse does not hold. Meister Eckhart got into trouble with the church hierarchy for writing, "I pray God [the God above all distinctions] that he may quit me of [the personal] 'God,' adorned with multiple virtues that are extensions of human ones." But though he insisted to the end that his thinking was orthodox, he admitted that he may have been imprudent in stating some things in ways that caused offense to people who did not understand them. He made amends by adding to his controversial statements these words: "If anyone does not find these truths in themselves, let them not worry about it." He fully understood that the esoterics' wider-angle lens does not necessarily make esoterics better people. Nor does it dispense with the church's need for exoterics. Everywhere in history exoterics far outnumber esoterics, and religious institutions run mostly on the energy they provide. In short, no shells, no kernels.

15. *Outside of Revelation's beam, we live in darkness.* It is a numinous darkness that lures, for we know that God sees it as light. He knows the way things are, but we grope our way. Such a confusing life and world, riven with contradictions and conflicting opinions that leave us not knowing what to think! At times we get glimmers of what it's all about, and at such times we see a kind of twilight zone around the edges of our darkness, but to cognition the darkness remains. We are born in ignorance, we live in ignorance, and we die in ignorance. As John of Ruysbroeck put it, "Our reason abides here with open eyes in this darkness, in abysmal ignorance. And in this darkness the abysmal splendor remains covered and hidden from us, for its overwhelming unfathomableness blinds our reason."

In relation to God we stand as less than a simple protein in a single cell on a human finger. Though living, that protein cannot know the cell in which it lives. How then could it conceive of the skin, the knuckle itself, or the finger's articulating joints, the intricacies of the ligaments, nerves, and muscles, the electronic biochemical processes of that finger of which it is a negligible part?

And even if it could, even if this simple protein could make that impossible leap, it could never conceive of the whole hand of which it is a part, the fingering for a guitar chord, the fist clenched in anger, the delicate touch needed for surgical repair of a heart. It is only a simple protein, an amino acid building block.

So much infinitely less are we literally, in this mass of the universe, and beyond it the Infinite. We are born in mystery, we live in mystery, and we die in mystery. It is not a dead mystery that bogs down in befuddlement. Religious mystery invites; it glows, lures, and excites, impelling us to enter its dazzling darkness ever more deeply. It is such mystery that Timothy had in mind when he told one of his churches, "Without any doubt the mystery of our religion is great." And it is why in the end prayer bumps into "the Cloud of Unknowing," a phrase used in the title of a fourteenth-century text that mystics dearly love. Prayer books pile negation on top of negation—invisible, unknowable, ineffable, incomprehensible, inconceivable—as their compilers stand dumbfounded in the presence of the Infinite Godhead.

But let me return to the luminous character of the darkness that we have been speaking of with two firsthand examples:

Friends once introduced my wife and me to a conversation piece that was resting on their coffee table. When activated, it displayed a medley of colors that shifted like a kaleidoscope when a key was pressed. One of our daughters was with us and exclaimed in delight: "I love it and I don't understand it at all, and that's why I believe in God."

I had something of the same experience when years ago I watched Edward R. Murrow interview Robert Oppenheimer. When Murrow had gotten past his questions about Los Alamos and Oppenheimer's captaining of the team that assembled the atomic bomb, Murrow asked what Oppenheimer was working on at the time that really excited him. Oppenheimer jumped up, went to the blackboard, and started covering it with squiggles that I assumed were equations. Talking passionately as he wrote, in less than a minute he had lost me completely, and I kept watching, glued to the television screen as never before, for I was being treated to the mysteries of frontier science.

In the preceding pages, I have presented the Christian worldview in fifteen component parts. Compressed into a single paragraph consisting of topic sentences, that worldview reads like this:

> The world is objectively there and intelligible. It is Infinite and includes the finite with its value-laden degrees, hierarchically ordered. As virtues ascend in the hierarchy, they meld into one another until their differences disappear in the Simple One. Evil features in finitude but not in the Absolute, and because the Absolute is all-powerful, in the end absolute perfection reigns. Human beings intersect the degrees of reality, but in them they appear inverted, as if seen on the surface of a glassy lake. We cannot comprehend the fullness of Reality on our own, but its outlines are revealed to us. The key to unlocking the truths of Revelation is symbolism. Knowing is both rational and intuitive, both concrete and abstract. After we have done our best to understand the world, it remains mysterious, but through the shrouds of mystery, we can dimly discern that it is perfect.

And now that same Christian worldview compressed even further, into a sentence: the world is perfect, and the human opportunity is to see that and conform to that fact.

If this doesn't sound distinctively Christian, the reason is that it isn't. It is the worldview of all authentic, which is to say *revealed*, religions.

During the fifteen years that I taught at the Massachusetts Institute of Technology, one of my colleagues was Noam Chomsky. Noam is best known to the public for his unflagging vigilance in targeting untruths in the media, but his profession is linguistics, where he revolutionized the field by discovering the universal grammar that is programmed into the human brain and from which the grammar of all spoken languages—English, Chinese, Swahili, what have you—conform. This first part of this book does the same thing with religions: it outlines the universal grammar of religion to which (in their various idioms) all religions conform.

Having completed this first part of the book, let me say a word to the reader. If you have not been trained in philosophy, this part of the book may have seemed dense and over your head at times, but take heart. As you get into Part Two, I think you will find that Part One established the fixed points on which the Christian story is stretched like canvas on a frame.

Two points remain to be made before Part Two opens.

First, Christianity began with the controversy over whether Jesus was or was not the Messiah, but Christians honor their heritage. I once heard a dean of the Harvard Divinity School—he was a New Testament scholar—say that the highest compliment you can pay a Christian is to say that he or she is an honorary Jew. I pricked up my ears because when I left Washington University some years earlier, the Jewish student organization, Hillel, made me an honorary Jew by presenting me with a Hillel lapel key at a farewell banquet they mounted for me. At the same time, however, Christians believe that their break with Judaism was justified—providential, in fact. How so?

By responding to God's invitation, the Jews had risen to a spiritual level that was head and shoulders above that of their neighbors. However, it was their religion; ethnically grounded in lineage, language, and history, it was not for other people. To this day Jews accept converts but do not seek them.

Thus, it is as if God thought: *The achievement of the Jews is too important to be kept to themselves. It needs to break out of its shell and be made available to the world at large. I will see to it that that is done.* The case exactly parallels Buddhism's split with Hinduism. Buddhism and Christianity are world religions, while Hinduism and Judaism are ethnic religions.

The second transitional point is this: Christianity entered history through God's revelation in Christ, but it does not end there. It moves on, through the New Testament, the church fathers, great theologians and saints; and, in fact, it is unending.

The Christian story that this book tells, however, deals only with the first millennium, during which (with the negligible exception of a few small pocket holdouts) Christianity was institutionally united and its creeds were set in place by ecumenical councils. That essential story deserves therefore to be considered classical Christianity, or the Great Tradition. Subsequent revelations are, in effect, "Christian midrashim," commentaries that interpret the "Christian Torah" but do not change it.

Part Two

———◆———

THE CHRISTIAN STORY

People tell themselves stories and then pour their lives into the stories they tell.

Anonymous

The message of Jesus is grounded in a metaphysics of peace, not the metaphysics of violence that Nietzsche mistook it for. The truth of that metaphysics cannot be proved, and it can be urged only by the beauty of the communal life of those who commit themselves to it.

Abridged from David Bentley
Hart, *The Beauty of the Infinite*

Of all the great religions, Christianity is the most widespread and has the largest number of adherents. Statistics on religions are notoriously unreliable, but current registries list almost one out of every three people on earth today as Christian, bringing the number into the neighborhood of two billion.

Nearly two thousand years of history have brought an astonishing diversity to this religion. From the majestic pontifical High Mass in St. Peter's to the quiet simplicity of a Quaker meeting; from the intellectual sophistication of Saint Thomas Aquinas to the moving simplicity of spirituals such as "Lord, I want to be a Christian"; from St. Paul's in London, the parish church of Great Britain, to Mother Teresa in the slums of Calcutta—all this is Christianity. From this dazzling and often bewildering complex, it is our task to describe Christianity's Great Tradition, which is to say its first millennium, before it divided into the Eastern Orthodox and Roman Catholic Churches. To this will be added, in Part Three, sections on the three major divisions of post-Reformation Christianity: Roman Catholicism, Eastern Orthodoxy, and Protestantism.

THE HISTORICAL JESUS

Christianity is basically a historical religion. That is to say, it is founded not on abstract principles but on concrete events, actual historical happenings. The most important of these is the life of a Jewish carpenter who, as has often been pointed out, was born in a stable, was executed as a criminal at age thirty-three, never traveled more than ninety miles from his birthplace, owned nothing, attended no school, marshaled no army, and instead of producing books did his only writing in the sand. Nevertheless, his birthday is kept across the world, and his death day sets a gallows against almost every skyline. Who was this man?

The biographical details of Jesus's life are meager. He was born in Palestine during the reign of Herod the Great, probably around 4 B.C.—The Christian calendar is probably off by several years. He grew up in or near Nazareth, presumably after the fashion of other normal Jews of the time. Of the "hidden years" between twelve and around thirty we know nothing. Accounts resume with his baptism by John, a dedicated prophet who was electrifying the region with his proclamation of God's coming judgment. In his early thirties Jesus had a teaching-healing career which lasted between one and three years and was focused largely in Galilee. In time he incurred the hostility of some of his own compatriots and the suspicion of Rome, which led to his crucifixion on the outskirts of Jerusalem.

From these facts that establish the framework of Jesus's life, we turn to the life he lived within that framework.

Minimally stated, Jesus was a charismatic wonder-worker who stood in a tradition that stretched back to the beginnings of Hebrew history. The prophets and seers who comprised that tradition mediated between the everyday world, on the one hand, and a Spirit world that enveloped it. From the Spirit world they drew power which they used both to help people and to challenge their ways. We shall expand this capsule characterization by considering successively (a) the Spirit world, to which Jesus was exceptionally connected and which powered his ministry; (b) his deployment of his Spirit-derived powers in the alleviation of human suffering; and (c) the new social order he felt commissioned to effect.

"The Spirit of the Lord Is upon Me"

According to Luke, Jesus opened his ministry by quoting the above statement from Isaiah and adding, "Today this scripture has been fulfilled." We must attend to this Spirit that Jesus experienced as empowering him, for there can be no understanding of his life and work if it is omitted.

In what has proved to be one of the twentieth century's most durable books about religion, *The Varieties of Religious Experience*, William James tells us that "in its broadest terms, religion says that there is an unseen order, and that our supreme good lies in rightful relations to it." Judaism is the story of a sustained and demanding dialogue of a chosen people with the unseen order that William James emphasizes. They called that order "Spirit" (from breath, as in aspirate), which in the opening verses of the Torah plays upon the primordial waters to create the world. Sensing it as intensely alive, they populated it with angels and archangels and also demons. Its center, however, was Yahweh, whom they envisioned personally: as shepherd, king, lord, father (and less commonly, mother), and lover. Though Spirit was typically pictured as being above the earth—images of ladders to Heaven are routine—that was only to stress its distinctness from and superiority over the mundane world. The two were not spatially separated and were in continuous interaction. God walked in the Garden of Eden, and "the whole earth is full of his glory."

Not only was Spirit not spatially removed; though invisible, it could be known. Often it would take the initiative and announce itself. It did this supremely to Moses on Mount Sinai, but it also spoke in a still small voice to Elijah, in lions' roars to other prophets, and in dramatic events such as the Exodus. Concurrently, human beings could take the initiative in contacting it. Fasting and solitude were means for doing so, and Jews who felt called would periodically remove themselves from the world's distractions to commune with the Divine through these aids. It would not be amiss to think of those early Jews as soaking themselves in Spirit during these vigils, for when they returned to the world they often gave evidence of having almost palpably absorbed Spirit and its attendant power.

That Jesus stood in the Jewish tradition of Spirit-filled mediators is the most important fact for understanding his historical career. His immediate predecessor in this tradition was John the Baptist, and it is a testament to John's spiritual power that it was his baptismal initiation of Jesus that opened Jesus's "third" or spiritual eye, through which he saw the heavens open and the Spirit of God descending upon him like a dove. Having descended on him, the Spirit "drove" Jesus into the wilderness, where, during forty days of prayer and fasting he consolidated the Spirit that had entered him and decisively faced down Satan's temptations to use his newly acquired power for his own personal ends.

"By the Spirit of God I Cast Out Demons"

Science has outgrown the "modern mistake" of discounting invisible realities, for physicists now know that the energy in one cubic centimeter of empty space is greater than the energy of all the matter in the known universe. It is not going too far to see that ratio as approximating the ratio of Spirit's power to ours, and the Spirit-filled personages in the Bible absorbed that power. To say that they were charismatic is to say they had power to attract people's attention—as we say today, they "had something." That *something* was the Spirit's infusion. The Bible repeatedly depicts those biblical personages as "filled with the power of the Spirit," which enabled them at times to influence even nature's workings. They healed diseases, cast out demons, and occasionally quelled storms, parted waters, and caused the dead to return to life. The Gospels attribute such powers to Jesus copiously. Again and again they report people flocking to him, drawn by his reputation for working wonders. "They brought to him all who were sick or possessed with demons, and the whole city was gathered together about the door." Modern mentality cannot accommodate such claims, but as the Introduction to this book indicated, that mentality is on the wane. Psychosomatic medicine and paranormal phenomena ranging from the powers of prayer, through telepathy and clairvoyance, to psychokenesis—a murky area to be sure, but one where incontrovertibly *something* goes on—have perforated the line between nature and supernature. In any case, on historical grounds it is virtually indisputable that Jesus was a miraculous healer and exorcist.

He could have been that—indeed, he could have been the most extraordinary figure in the stream of Jewish charismatic healers—without attracting more than local attention. What made him outlive his time and place was the way he used the Spirit that coursed through him not just to heal individuals but to heal humanity, beginning with his own people.

The Christian Story

"Thy Kingdom Come, on Earth"

Politically, the position of the Jews in Jesus's time was desperate. They had been in servitude to Rome for the better part of a century and, along with being deprived of freedom, were being taxed beyond endurance. Existing responses to their predicament were four, depending on whether one was a Sadducee, an Essene, a Pharisee, or a Zealot.

The *Sadducees,* who were relatively well off, favored making the best of a bad situation and accommodated themselves to Hellenistic culture and Roman rule.

The other positions hoped for change. All three recognized that the change would have to be effected by Yahweh, and all assumed that the Jews needed to do something that would prompt his intervention.

Two of the three were renewal movements. The *Essenes* considered the world too corrupt to allow for Judaism to renew itself within it, so they dropped out. Withdrawing into property-sharing communes, they devoted themselves to lives of disciplined piety. The *Pharisees,* on the other hand, remained within society and sought to revitalize Judaism through adhering strictly to the Mosaic law, especially its holiness code.

Representatives of the fourth position have been referred to as *Zealots,* but it is doubtful that they were sufficiently organized to deserve a name. Despairing that the needed change could occur without armed force, they launched sporadic acts of resistance that culminated in the catastrophic revolt of A.D. 66–70, which led to the second destruction of the Temple in Jerusalem.

Into this political cauldron Jesus introduced a fifth option. Unlike the Sadducees, he wanted change. Unlike the Essenes, he remained in the world. Unlike the advocates of armed rebellion, he extolled peacemaking and urged that even enemies be loved. It was the Pharisees that Jesus stood closest to, for the difference between them was one of emphasis only. The Pharisees stressed Yahweh's holiness while Jesus stressed Yahweh's compassion, but the Pharisees would have been the first to insist that Yahweh was also compassionate, and Jesus that Yahweh was holy. On the surface the difference appears to be small, but it proved to be too large for a single religion to accommodate. How so?

Grounding themselves in the understanding of Yahweh as majestic holiness, the Pharisees went on to affirm the accepted version of Jewish self-understanding. Being holy himself, Yahweh wanted to hallow the world as well, and to accomplish this aim he selected the Jews to plant for him, as it were, a beachhead of holiness in human history. On Mount Sinai he had prescribed a holiness code, faithful observance of which would make of the Hebrews "a nation of priests." Yahweh's instruction to them, "You shall be holy, as I the Lord your God am holy," became the Pharisees' watchword. It was laxity in the observance of the holiness code that had reduced the Jews to their degraded state, they believed, and only the wholehearted return to it would reverse that state.

Much of this Jesus subscribed to, but there was an important feature of the holiness program he found unacceptable: the lines that it drew between people. Beginning by categorizing acts and things as clean or unclean (foods and their preparation, for example), the holiness code went on to categorize people according to whether they respected those distinctions. The result was a social structure riven with barriers: between people who were clean and unclean, pure and defiled, sacred and profane, Jew and Gentile, righteous and sinner. Jesus was painfully aware that in this imperfect world even the best of societies have cracks through which people fall to become the scum of the earth, the lost, the rejected, the outcast, the marginalized, the effaced, the defeated, the forsaken. Social barriers widen these cracks and are therefore an affront to the God who spreads his mantle over his children universally. So Jesus parleyed with tax collectors, dined with outcasts and sinners, socialized with prostitutes, and healed on the Sabbath when compassion prompted his doing so. This made him a social prophet, challenging the boundaries of the existing order and advocating an alternative vision of the human community.

It cannot be said too often that Jesus was deeply Jewish. At the same time he stood in sharp tension with Judaism.

In passing, this tension can be seen as an important aspect of his Jewishness, for no religion has encouraged internal criticism to the extent that Judaism has. The most memorable lecture on Judaism that I have heard was by a rabbi who drew me to his lecture by its improbable title, "Whatever Happened to Jewish Disputatiousness?" The lecture was delivered around the middle of the twentieth century, and it voiced his apprehension that the creation of the state of Israel had caused Jews to close ranks in support of that state to the point where they were papering over differences when, in the rabbi's view, it was diversity that had kept Judaism vibrant.

To conclude the point that was interrupted by the above digression, Jesus saw the holiness code and the distinctions that followed from it as having been needed to lift the Jews to a purity that surpassed that of their neighbors, making them in effect a chosen people. However, his own encounter with God led him to conclude that, as practiced in his time, the purity system had created social divisions that compromised God's impartial, all-encompassing love for everyone. This put him at odds with religious leaders, but his protest did not prevail. It did, however, attract enough attention to alarm the Roman authorities, and as we shall see, this led to his arrest and execution on charges of treason.

Thereafter the future of the "Jesus people" lay with the wider world. In time Christians (who first inherited that name at Antioch) came to read this development positively. As was noted at the close of Part One, to their eyes God's revelation to the Jews was too important to be confined to a single ethnic group. The mission of Jesus and his followers had been to crack the shell of Judaism in which Revelation was encased and release that Revelation to a ready and waiting world. Putting it this way does not cancel the need for a continuing Jewish presence. Until the world is redeemed, there will always be need for the witness of a nation of priests.

THE CHRIST OF FAITH

How does one move from Jesus's life to the Christ whom his followers came to believe was God in human form? His disciples did not reach that conclusion before Jesus's death, but even in his lifetime we can see that a momentum was building in its direction. Having sketched the facts of Jesus's life, we turn now to the way he came through to his disciples. The headings in the preceding "The Historical Jesus" section were spoken by Jesus himself, whereas from here on they are his disciples' descriptions of him.

We are on firmer ground here, for if the Gospels disclose little in the way of historical facts, they are transparent regarding Jesus's impact on his disciples. This impact derived from what he did, what he said, and who he was. We will consider the three successively.

"He Went About Doing Good"

The Gospels vibrate with wonder at Jesus's actions. The pages of Mark especially are peppered with accounts of miracles. We have seen that these impressed multitudes, but it would be a mistake to place our emphasis there. For one thing, Jesus did not publicize his miracles. He never used them as devices to strong-arm people into believing in him. Satan tempted Jesus to do so, but we have seen that in his forty days of soul-searching in the wilderness, Jesus triumphed over that temptation. Almost all of his extraordinary deeds were performed quietly, apart from crowds, and as a demonstration of the power of faith. Moreover, other writings of the times abound in miracles, but this did not lead witnesses to deify their agents. They merely credited the miracle workers with unusual power—with *siddhi*, as the Indians would say.

We get a better perspective on Jesus's actions if we place the emphasis where one of his disciples did. Once, in addressing a group, Peter found it necessary to compress into a narrow compass what Jesus did during his lifetime. His summary was, "He went about doing good"—a simple epitaph, but a moving one. Circulating easily and without affectation among ordinary people and social misfits, healing them, counseling them, helping them out of chasms of despair, Jesus went about doing good. People tend to dislike being interrupted, but it was impossible to interrupt Jesus because he simply dealt with what was at hand. He did so with such single-mindedness and effectiveness that those who were with him found their estimate of him persistently modulating to a new key. They found themselves thinking that if divine goodness were to manifest itself in human form, this is how it would behave.

The theme of this section is "doing good," and it is worth exploring it a little more. There are many ways of doing good. Several were just mentioned, but a short catalogue can round out the picture. Healing physical afflictions has been dealt with. Helping people understand how they should live is another important benefaction. In the middle of the twentieth century, one of the best-known psychiatrists was William Sheldon of Columbia University's College of Physicians and Surgeons. Looking back on his career he said that "continued observation in clinical practice leads almost inevitably to the conclusion that deeper and more fundamental than sexuality, deeper than the craving for social power, deeper even than the desire for possessions, there is a still more generalized and universal craving in the human makeup. It is craving for the knowledge of the right direction—for orientation." Jesus gave people that knowledge. (This will be dealt with at some length in the next section.)

A third way in which Jesus "did good" involved people's need for companionship. Companionship is very different from company. At a cocktail party one can feel isolated even when people keep making contact and chatter inconsequently—a point David Riesman made famous with the title of his book *The Lonely Crowd*. The heart of companionship is bonding—two or more people feeling bonded to one another in mutual affection and esteem. People felt bonded to Jesus simply by being in his presence, it seems. One thinks of Socrates' disciples, who lived for the times they could be together with him. The phrase "bids them welcome," said of the Buddha, also comes to mind: whatever the cast or circumstances of the people who came to the Buddha, he bid them welcome—which is to say, accepted them.

"Never Spoke Man Thus"

It was not only what Jesus did, however, that made his contemporaries elevate him. It was also what he said.

There has been a great deal of controversy over the originality of Jesus's teachings. The responsible conclusion is that individually they can all be found in the Torah or its commentaries. However, if you take them as a whole, they have an urgency, an ardent, vivid quality, an abandon, and above all a complete absence of second-rate material that makes them refreshingly new.

Apart from its content, the language of Jesus has proved to be a fascinating study in itself, reminding us that, as the saying goes, the medium is part of the message. If simplicity, concentration, heart-stopping eloquence, and the sense of what is vital are marks of great religious speech and literature, these qualities alone would make Jesus's words immortal. But this is just the beginning. His words carry an extravagance of which mere wise men, tuned to the importance of nuances and balanced judgments, are incapable. Their passionate quality led one New Testament scholar to coin a word for Jesus's language, calling it "gigantesque." If your hand offends you, says Jesus, cut if off. If your eye stands between you and the best, gouge it out. Jesus talks of camels that squeeze their humps through needles' eyes. His characters go around with timbers protruding from their eyes while they look for tiny specks in the eyes of others. Jesus talks of people whose outer lives are stately mausoleums while their inner lives stink of decaying corpses. This is not simply language tooled for rhetorical effect. It is language, as was just noted, that is integral to the message itself, prompted by the driving urgency of the gospel. When Flannery O'Connor, a southern Catholic writer, was asked why her characters were so often grotesques, she replied, "To the hard of hearing you have to shout, and to the nearly blind you have to draw large and startling figures." Jesus's startling analogies can be explained only by the strength of his passion for truth and his determination to shock his listeners into realizing that they were settling for far, far less.

An anecdote can throw light on this. On the beach of Venice, California—a beach enclosed within Los Angeles—there used to be a tourist attraction called Muscle Beach. On hot summer evenings bronze and blonde god-and-goddess bodybuilders would pour out of their dreary offices and, skimpily attired, besport themselves in their exercises to the amazed delight of the onlookers. During the Vietnam War, the draft board rejected one of the muscle-builders because he had expanded his biceps to the point where they were too large to slip through the sleeves of a G.I. shirt, and the army wasn't about to tailor a custom-made outfit for one soldier.

One evening on Muscle Beach a spectator was rash enough to accuse the man of being a draft dodger. The enraged accused seized his taunter by the front of his leather jacket, lifted him off his feet, and shook him at arm's length so violently that it looked as if his flopping head was going to fall off his neck. Setting the man back on his feet, the muscle-builder turned and walked away in disgust.

The analogy may be strained, but it is as if that was what Jesus was trying to do to his crowds of listeners: lift them off their conventional feet and shake his truths into them.

A second arresting feature of Jesus's language was its invitational style. Instead of telling people what to do or what to believe, he invited them to *see* things differently, confident that if they did so their behavior would change. This called for working with people's imagination more than with their reason or their will. If listeners were to accept his invitation, the place to which they were being invited would have to seem real to them. So, because the reality his hearers were most familiar with consisted of concrete particulars, Jesus began with those particulars. He spoke of mustard seeds and rocky soil, of servants and masters, of weddings and wine. These specifics grounded his teachings, for he was speaking of things that his hearers' daily lives were made of. But then, having won their confidence by assuring them that he knew what he was talking about, Jesus rode the momentum of their confidence and gave it a startling, subversive twist. That phrase, "momentum of confidence," is important, for its deepest meaning is that Jesus located the authority for his teachings not in himself or in God-as-removed but in his hearers' own hearts. My teachings are true, he said in effect, not because they come from me, or even from God through me, but because (against all conventional odds) in your deepest selves you *know* that they are true.

So what did Jesus use his gigantesque, invitational language to say? Not a great deal, as far as the records report; everything the New Testament quotes him as saying can be spoken in two hours. Yet those sayings may be the most repeated in the whole of history. "Love your neighbor as yourself." "Love your enemies." "Whatever you wish that men would do to you, do to them." "Come unto me, all you that labor and are heavy laden, and I will give you rest." "You shall know the truth, and the truth shall make you free."

Most of the time, however, Jesus told stories that we call parables: of buried treasure, of sowers who go out to sow, of pearl merchants, of a good Samaritan, of a man who had two sons, one of whom blew his inheritance on a binge and found himself cadging scraps from the pigs. People who heard these stories were moved to exclaim, "This man speaks with authority!" and "Never spoke man thus!"

They were astonished, and with reason. If *we* are not, it is because we have heard Jesus's teachings so often that their edges have been worn smooth, dulling their glaring subversiveness. If we could recover their original impact, we too would be startled. Their beauty would not paper over the fact that they are "hard sayings," presenting a scheme of values so counter to the usual as to shake us like the seismic collision of tectonic plates.

We are told that we are not to resist evil but to turn the other cheek. The world assumes that evil must be resisted by every means available. We are told to love our enemies and bless those who curse us. The world assumes that friends are to be loved and enemies hated. We are told that the sun rises on the just and the unjust alike. The world considers this indiscriminating; it would like to see dark clouds withholding sunshine from evil people. We are told that outcasts and harlots enter the kingdom of God before many who are perfunctorily righteous. Unfair, we protest; respectable people should head the procession. We are told that the gate to salvation is narrow. The world would prefer it to be wide. We are told to be as carefree as birds and flowers. The world counsels prudence. We are told that it is more difficult for the rich to enter the kingdom than for a camel to pass through a needle's eye. The world honors wealth. We are told that the happy people are those who are meek, who weep, who are merciful and pure in heart. The world assumes that it is the rich, the powerful, and the wellborn who should be happy. In all, a wind of freedom blows through these teachings that frightens the world and makes us want to deflect their effect by postponement—not yet, not yet! H. G. Wells was evidently right: either there was something mad about this man, or our hearts are still too small for his message.

Again we must come back to what those teachings were about. Everything that came from Jesus's lips worked like a magnifying glass to focus human awareness on the two most important facts about life: God's overwhelming love of humanity, and the need for people to accept that love and let it flow through them in the way water passes without obstruction through a sea anemone. In experiencing God as infinite love bent on people's salvation, Jesus was an authentic child of Judaism; he differed, we have seen, only in not allowing the post-Exilic holiness code to impede God's compassion. Time after time, as in his story of the shepherd who risked ninety-nine sheep to go after the one that had strayed, Jesus tried to convey God's absolute love for every single human being and for everything God has created. The hairs of each head are counted. God notices the death of each and every sparrow. And not even Solomon in all his glory was as majestically arrayed as the lilies of the field. If the infinity of God's love pierces to the core of a being, only one response is possible— unobstructed gratitude for the wonders of God's grace.

Stated only slightly differently, the only way to make sense of Jesus's extraordinary admonitions as to how people should live is to see them as cut from his understanding of the God who loves human beings absolutely and unconditionally, without pausing to calculate their worth or due. We are to give others our cloak as well as our coat if they need it. Why? Because God has given us what we need many times over. We are to go with others the second mile. Again, why? Because we know, deeply, overwhelmingly, that God has borne with us for far longer stretches. Why should we love not only our friends but also our enemies, and pray for those who persecute us? "So that you may be children of your Father in heaven; for he makes his sun to rise on the evil and on the good, and sends rain on the unrighteous as well as the righteous." We must be perfect, as God is perfect. We say Jesus's ethic is perfectionistic—a polite word for unrealistic—because it asks that we love unreservedly. But the reason we consider that unrealistic, Jesus would have answered, is because we do not allow ourselves to experience the constant, unstinted love that flows from God to us. If we did experience it, problems would still arise. To which of the innumerable needy should limited supplies of coats and cloaks be given? When we run into mean bullies, are we to lie down and let them tromp over us? Jesus offered no rule book to obviate hard choices. What he argued for was for the stance from which we should approach those choices. All we can say in advance as we face the demands of our extravagantly complicated world is that we should respond to our neighbors—all of them that we think might be affected by our actions—not in proportion to what we see as their due but in proportion to their need. The cost to us personally should count for nothing.

Jesus draws his teachings together in the Sermon on the Mount. Seeing that a large crowd has assembled, he leads them up the slope of a mountain and teaches them, beginning with the Beatitudes, which are worth quoting in full:

Blessed are the poor in spirit, for theirs is the kingdom of
  heaven.
Blessed are those who mourn, for they will be comforted.
Blessed are the meek, for they will inherit the earth.
Blessed are those who hunger and thirst after righteous-
  ness, for they will be filled.
Blessed are the merciful, for they will receive mercy.

Blessed are the pure in heart, for they will see God.

Blessed are the peacemakers, for they will be called the children of God.

Blessed are those who are persecuted for righteousness' sake, for theirs is the kingdom of heaven.

Blessed are you when people revile you and persecute you and utter all kinds of evil against you falsely on my account. Rejoice and be glad, for in the same way they persecuted the prophets who were before you.

We learn from these sayings that blessedness—beatitude—is not unalloyed happiness. It is paradoxical happiness, wherein the sorrow is not eliminated but is enfolded and transmuted by God's all-permeating love. In blessedness the spear of suffering is enveloped in a shaft of light. The light shines in darkness, which does not consume it.

In the third beatitude, the meek are not those who abase themselves. Putting on the breastplate and helmet of God, they do battle with principalities and powers; but they do so without wishing to *supplant* them, for it is power per se, power as such, that is the enemy. Weakness that does not covet worldly strength—in short, meekness—has the strength to inherit the earth. Not, however, this mundane earth, for "my kingdom is not of this world."

The other most memorable part of the Sermon on the Mount is the Lord's Prayer.

Jesus prayed a lot. In the way wind and water give shape to dunes and valleys, Jesus fashioned his human nature and created it in the way God fashioned Adam in his own image and likeness. For Jesus's human nature wasn't simply an empty jug into which his incarnation automatically flowed. Prayer brought things into his human nature that were not there before.

"The longest way 'round is the shortest way home," Taoists say, and their saying prompts the following anecdote: Two years ago I flew to Chicago to attend a conference on unusual capacities of the human mind. The first speaker was a medical school professor. He began by saying that he was not a believer, he was an atheist; however he *was* a conscientious medical instructor, and as such he kept a close watch on what helped to heal his patients. He then went into a pendulum swing that characterized the rest of his talk—back and forth from first-hand reports to calling the audience's attention to the information he projected onto an overhead screen that was behind him.

His first anecdotal report was of a patient with a brain tumor that had reached a size that was too large to be surgically removed. He broke the unhappy news to the patient's family, and told them to take the patient home and give him their loving care for the remaining week or two of his life. Three weeks later the dismissed patient strode into his office with two of his family saying that he thought his physician would be interested in knowing that he was well. A brain scan confirmed that the size of the cancerous tumor was dramatically reduced. Dumbfounded, he physician asked the family what they had done that might account for the recovery. "We prayed fervently and almost constantly," they told him, adding, "as did all our relatives and the members of our church." The physician thanked them for coming back to him and told them to keep on praying.

Then he turned on his flashlight and aimed its red pointer-dot at the overhead screen, explaining that its boxes showed the results of the twenty-four best-researched studies on prayer that had been conducted. The success scores varied from the fifties to the nineties, but all were above average. More firsthand reports and references to the studies consumed the remainder of the hour up to his conclusion. He had stopped keeping track of ongoing studies of prayer—that prayer works he considered proved—and was turning his research to how it works.

"Good luck, buddy," I thought to myself, adding that God's ways are not our ways. However, there is something that, although it does not explain how prayer works, may throw some light on the subject.

One of the objectives of this book is to present the Christian story in contemporary idiom—which is to say, in the light of the best we now know, including science. The most important scientific discovery of all time—anticipated by Einstein, worked out in Bell's Theorem, and experimentally confirmed by the EPR (Einstein-Podosky-Rosen) experiment—proves that the universe is "non-local."

Described in everyday language, the story is this: Particles have spins. In paired particles, when one particle spins downward the other spins upward. Now, separate the two—distance is irrelevant; it can be an inch or to the edge of the universe—and when one particle goes into a downspin, simultaneously the other spins upward. For prayer, nonlocality suggests that the person praying and the person being prayed for are closer than side by side. Distance doesn't apply—they are in the same spaceless mathematical point. When the pray-er plunges deep down into his praying self, his prayer spins downward, so to speak, and spins its recipient upward. When Jesus prayed all night, and during the day, he was "spun upward" by placing himself in the presence of his Father who so loved the world that he "spun down"—into his Incarnation, Jesus—and transformed him.

The prayer Jesus taught the multitude is known as the Lord's Prayer, *adonai* (lord) being the Jews' stand-in for the tetragramaton YHVH, the name of God that is too sacred to write or pronounce. The prayer is addressed to the *abba* (father) of us all, and the full salutation, "Our Father who art in heaven" makes it clear that it carries no gender connotations, for this is no human father: it is God himself, who is *beyond* gender.

Though Jesus would have found gender inappropriate in referring to God, familial terms were required because family relationships are the most intimate relationships we enjoy. To speak of God's love for his children and Jesus's longing to gather the children of Jerusalem to him as a hen gathers her brood under her wings came naturally. At the same time, however, Jesus came down hard on the difference between *God's* family—in which everyone is brother and sister—and the *human* family. This is important enough to dwell on for a moment.

Of all of Jesus's "hard sayings," the hardest for many Christians to come to terms with are those that relate to the human family. Well aware of the offense these teachings would cause, Jesus introduced these dicta by warning his hearers that he had "come not to bring peace, but a sword." For

- "I have come to set a man against his father and a daughter against her mother-in-law, and one's foes will be members of his own household."

- Further, "Whoever comes to me and does not hate father and mother, wife and children, brothers and sisters cannot be my disciple."

- When a would-be follower of Jesus asked that he first be permitted to go home and bury his father, Jesus told him to "let the dead bury the dead."

To understand these words we need to understand the Mediterranean culture in which they were spoken. Virtually no other peoples had the power over their children that the Romans had. The paterfamilias could discard a child at birth—simply throw it away. If he chose to keep it, he had the power to have it killed at any moment. Jesus was dead set against this absolute, dictatorial, coercive power of the human father, and it was an important part of his mission to replace it with the heavenly Father and his family. On an occasion when he was in a crowded household and was told that his mother and brothers were outside, and was asked if he would like to go out and greet them, he asked, rhetorically, who his mother and brothers were. He supplied his own answer: "those who do my Father's will." As for letting the dead bury the dead, it was understood in the Roman world that sons were to support their fathers until they buried them, which meant that it might be years before Jesus's would-be disciples could join him.

In its entirety, the Lord's Prayer reads:

Our Father who art in Heaven, hallowed be thy name. Thy kingdom come; thy will be done, on earth as it is in heaven. Give us this day our daily bread, and forgive us our trespasses as we forgive those who trespass against us. And lead us not into temptation [if we adhere to the Aramaic, this would read "lead us not into confusion, or mistaken priorities"], but deliver us from evil; [to which the Christians, in saying the prayer, add] for thine is the kingdom and the power and the glory forever. Amen.

We have spoken of what Jesus did and what he said, but these implicit and explicit expressions would not have been enough to edge his disciples toward the conclusion that he was divine had it not been for a third factor: what Jesus *was*. At first glance it might seem that "what" Jesus was should read "who" he was, but "what" is correct, for what follows is about levels of being, not personalities.

"We Have Seen His Glory"

"There is in the world," writes Dostoyevsky, "only one figure of absolute beauty: Christ. That infinitely lovely figure is an infinite marvel."

Certainly, the most impressive thing about the teachings of Jesus is not that he taught them but that he lived them. From the accounts that we have, his entire life was one of humility, self-giving, and love that sought not its own. The supreme evidence of his humility may be that he didn't tell Matthew, Mark, and Luke precisely what he thought of himself, though to his beloved disciple John he disclosed himself transparently. For the rest, his concern was not what people thought of him but what they thought of God—God's nature and God's will for their lives. By indirection, to be sure, this does tell us something about Jesus's self-image, but only that he esteemed himself to be less than God: "Why do you call me good? Don't you know that only God is good?"

It is impossible to listen to what Jesus said about selflessness without sensing how free of pride he himself was. Similarly with sincerity: what he said on the subject could have been said only by someone whose life was uncluttered by deceit and guile. Truth to him was like the life-giving air we breathe.

Through the pages of the Gospels Jesus emerges as a man of strength and integrity who bore about him no strangeness at all save the strangeness of perfection. He liked people and they liked him in turn. In fact, they loved him; they loved him intensely and they loved him in numbers. Drawn to him not only by his charisma and his healing powers but by the compassion that flowed from him, they surrounded him, flocked about him, and followed him. He stood by the Sea of Galilee and they pressed so hard that he had to speak to them from a boat. He set out for the day and a crowd of several thousand accumulated, missing lunch, staying on until suddenly they discovered that they were famished.

People responded to Jesus, but equally he responded to them. He felt their needs, whether they were rich or poor, young or old, saints or sinners. We have seen that he ignored the barriers that social conventions erected between people. He knew that people needed to belong, and he told those who could afford to give banquets to invite "the poor, cripples, the lame and the blind." He loved children and he hated injustice because of what it did to those he called, tenderly, "the least of these." (There was nothing sentimental in all this. His anger could blaze furiously, as when he upset tables and drove money-changers out of temples.) Above all he hated hypocrisy, because it hid people from themselves and precluded the authenticity he sought to build into relationships. All of this came together in a way that made those who knew him best conclude that here was a man in whom the human ego had all but disappeared. An ego existed in that his body was not the body of others, and his thoughts and feelings too were distinctively his own. But his ego-boundaries were perforated, so to speak, enabling him to exemplify his admonition to "rejoice with those who rejoice and weep with those who mourn."

The needs and dangers of the ego are central enough to the human condition to warrant a brief discussion of the subject. We can begin by noting with psychologists that ego-strength is good, whereas egotism, self-centeredness, is bad; and it is in this latter sense that I use the word "ego" here. Fond of paradoxes, Zen masters say that zero equals infinity ($0=\infty$), a koan the solution of which is to make "0" stand for zero-ego. Paul said that Jesus emptied himself not only of self-consciousness but also of divinity: "Jesus Christ, though he was in the form of God, did not regard equality with God as something to be exploited, but emptied himself, taking the form of a slave, being born in human likeness. And being found in human form, he humbled himself and became obedient to the point of death—even death on the cross."

Released from self-consciousness, Jesus's self expanded to let in the world in the way a downstream river swells when the sluice gates of a dam are opened. He now experienced the world unrestrictedly, vividly, objectively, and accurately, noticing things that other people overlook. And he was free because he was his own master—independent, self-reliant, authentic, and autonomous. Ego is dualistic; it sets itself against a not-self, as subject opposing objects. In doing so it deprives itself of the comfort and rest that a freed self enjoys, for the ego is a stumbling block, and stumbling over it is annoying and peace-inhibiting.

In a different metaphor, egotistic smudges obscure our vision of what's before us, just as smudges of dirt obscure rays of sunlight shining through a window. Jesus wiped away all smudges of ego to attune his will perfectly to God's will. His love for his Father was so complete that no love remained for him to squander on himself. Thus emptied of self, what remained was a vacuum to be filled by God. As Angelus Silesius, a seventeenth-century German mystical poet, put the point,

> *O God, whose boundless love and joy*
> *are present everywhere,*
> *He cannot come to visit you*
> *unless you are not there.*

This is true, but even when there are no smudges and a window pane admits sunlight undiminished, the incoming rays are not the sun itself. So too, God the Father remains distinct from God the Son; the "two natures" of Christ are not conflated. In the lyric cry of the early church: "We have seen his glory, full of grace and truth."

In one dramatic incident recorded in the New Testament, Peter, John, and James saw this glory with their physical eyes. On Mount Tabor—the Mount of Transfiguration, as it came to be called—they watched Jesus's face change while he was praying, and saw his clothes shine with dazzling brilliance. What they were privileged to see there, as if through a prism, was a condensation of the glory that shone through Jesus's entire life.

Centuries later, Shakespeare converted into poetry what has been said about that glory in this whole section:

Some say that ever 'gainst that season comes
Wherein our Savior's birth is celebrated,
The bird of dawning singeth all night long;
And then, they say, no spirit can walk abroad;
The nights are wholesome; then no planets strike,
No fairy tales, nor witch hath power to charm,
So hallow'd and so gracious is the time.

HOLY WEEK

Going back to the Jesus of history and rounding out the recorded events of Jesus's life, as the last Passover season he was to experience approached we are told that "he steadfastly set his face toward Jerusalem." The word "steadfastly" here is well chosen; it registers the determination he needed to face what was in store for him, for the Roman oppression was unbearable and the disputes among the Jews as to how to deal with it were at the boiling point. The Pharisees in particular were alarmed by the growing number of Jesus's adherents, and a showdown seemed likely.

Palm Sunday

Shortly after Jesus arrived in Jerusalem, a procession spontaneously formed, with Jesus riding on a donkey and onlookers cheering him on and waving palm fronds with which they also lined the path before him. A G. K. Chesterton poem captures the spirit of the occasion by reporting it through, of all things, the eyes of a donkey:

When fishes flew and forests walked
And figs grew upon thorn,
Some moment when the moon was blood
Then surely I was born.

With monstrous head and sickening cry
And ears like errant wings,
The devil's walking parody
On all four-footed things.

The tattered outlaw of the earth,
Of ancient crooked will;
Starve, scourge, deride me: I am dumb,
I keep my secret still.

Fools! For I also had my hour;
One far fierce hour and sweet:
There was a shout about my ears,
And palms before my feet.

The hosannas about the donkey's ears meant "Save now!" But of course the kind of salvation the onlookers were hoping for didn't happen.

Daily in Holy Week Jesus went to the Temple to pray and exhort, and on one occasion, as was previously noted, he drove money-changers out of the Temple courtyard for turning the sanctuary into a den of thieves when it was God's will that it be "a house of prayer for all nations."

Maundy Thursday

On the day before the Passover, Jesus and his disciples had their last meal together. Before eating, Jesus wrapped a towel around his waist, took a basin, and against his disciples' protests washed their feet and gave them a new commandment, that they love one another. If his injunction had stopped there it would not have been new, but when he added "as I have loved you"—totally, completely, unreservedly—it *was* new, and the day entered the church calendar as Maundy Thursday, from the Latin *mondeo,* "I command."

After the footwashing, they all sat down for their Last Supper together. In breaking the bread, Jesus told his disciples that it was a portent of the impending breaking of his body, and that the wine he blessed was a symbol of the blood he would be shedding. He asked them to repeat the meal after he was gone "in remembrance of me." The word "remembrance" is laden with symbolism, for to re-member is to reassemble parts that have been sundered. Thus, after death tore Jesus from his disciples, he would be back with them when they re-membered him in reenacting this Last Supper.

> And is it true? And is it true,
> This most tremendous tale of all,
> That God was Man in Palestine
> And lives today in Bread and Wine?
>   John Betjeman

The Night on the Mount of Olives

After the supper the group retired to the Mount of Olives to pray. At some point Jesus told his disciples to stop, that he would go alone into the Garden of Gethsemane, but they were to keep vigil with him through the night. A hymn recalls the succeeding hours:

> 'Tis midnight, and on Olive's brow
> The star is dimmed that brightly shone.
> 'Tis midnight in the garden now.
> The suff'ring Savior prays alone.

Sensing what was in store for him, Jesus threw himself on the ground in agony and prayed that, if it was possible, "this cup" might pass from him. He was experiencing a yawning gap between subject and object, between himself and his Father. As he would again be in his sense of abandonment on the cross, he was deep in the valley of the shadow of death, in a dark night of the soul, a virtual hell with its sense that God had died. Jesus's human nature required that he traverse a great void on the way to his resurrection. An African-American spiritual takes note of this:

Jesus walked the lonesome valley,
He had to walk it by himself;
Oh, nobody else could walk it for him,
He had to walk it by himself.

However, it was only God as object (the God he was praying to), not God as subject (the incarnated God that he was) that had deserted him, for to his supplication that the cup we spared him he added, "Nevertheless, not my will but yours be done."

The Crucifixion

We do not know the exact steps that led to Jesus's crucifixion the next day, but we have a lot of general information.

In the Passover season Jerusalem was a tinderbox that could burst into flames at any moment. As many Jews as possibly could crowded into the city to celebrate the highest holy day of the year, and the city was abuzz with clashing arguments as to the best way of dealing with the Roman oppression. Pontius

Pilate, Rome's deputy, was on the alert for uprisings that might trigger rebellion, and his soldiers were instructed to move quickly on potential troublemakers. Jesus, with his rising tide of popularity, was high on the list. In the dead of night, soldiers took Jesus from the Garden of Gethsemane and the next day Pilate put him on trial.

Part of Pilate's strategy for keeping a lid on the cauldron was to crucify several political suspects and lawbreakers on the day of preparation for the Passover, as a warning. These were public events that attracted huge crowds. It was surely no accident that the timing of Jesus's trial made him a good candidate for this role.

The earliest accounts we have of Jesus's trial were written forty years after the event took place, and they reflect the conflict that grew out of the dispute among the Jews as to whether Jesus was or was not the Messiah ("Christ," in Hebrew). The difference was irreconcilable, and from it Christianity emerged as a distinct religion. Naturally the Jews felt betrayed and did everything they could to suppress the heresy. This issue funnels directly into Saul/Paul's life and work, but the point I want to make here is that the Gospel accounts are filtered through the suffering that Christians had endured to win their independence. From Mark to Matthew to Luke to John, the Gospels shift the responsibility for Jesus's execution from Rome to the Jews. "The crowd" and "people as a whole" who clamor for Jesus's death in Mark become in Luke "the chief priests and the crowds," and in John "the Jews," "the Jews," the "Jews," "the Jews"—*Jews* being repeated four times for emphasis. Obviously everyone in Jerusalem was a Jew except its rulers, but the Gospels turn the Jews into a faction that secured Jesus's death.

Part of Pilate's governing strategy was to balance a public crucifixion with release of another criminal. When (finding no fault with Jesus) Pilate proposed that the man to be freed that particular Passover be Jesus, "the Jews" demanded that it be Barabbas instead.

Here we see a specific way in which the Gospels use subsequent history to press their charges against "the Jews." The disastrous rebellion of 67–70 led to the destruction of the Second Temple and Barabbas had preached rebellion. Therefore (as the Gospels tell the story), in asking for his release "the Jews" had in effect brought the Temple down on their own heads.

Because anti-Semitism has continued right down to today, the foregoing needed to be said, for there is no way to take the Gospel accounts of the crucifixion at face value without their sounding anti-Semitic. Placing them in their historical context and seeing them as a reaction to the persecution Christians were suffering from the Jews when the Gospels were written—as severe as their persecutions of the Jews would be when they got the upper hand—is the only way to fold the Gospels into Christian revelation.

Condemned, Jesus and two thieves were scourged and taken to the Hill of the Skull, Golgotha, outside Jerusalem, and nailed to their crosses around noon. Darkness came over the land, and hanging from his cross Jesus cried out in agony, *"Eli, Eli, lama sabachthani,"* which is, "Father, Father, why have you forsaken me?" Later he added, "Father, forgive them, for they do not know what they are doing," and at the end he cried out, "It is finished."

In mid-afternoon a spear was thrust into his side to determine whether he was dead. Christians cherish every detail of this scene, which won for them their salvation, and they keep turning it over and over in their minds and songs, as these lines from the hymn "Rock of Ages" attest:

Let the water and the blood,
From thy wounded side which flowed,
Be of sin the double cure,
Save from wrath and make me pure.

That stanza is not individualized. It can be sung in the first-person plural—*we*, the entire congregation, are voicing this supplication in unison. But in the closing stanza, which was quoted in Part One of this book, the implied "we" changes to an explicit "I":

While I draw this fleeting breath,
When my eyes shall close at death,
When I rise to worlds unknown,
And behold thee on thy throne;
Rock of Ages, cleft for me,
Let me hide myself in thee.

When it was determined that Jesus had died, his body was taken from the cross and placed in a cavelike sepulcher that an onlooker, Joseph of Arimathea, offered.

The handful of disciples and friends who had fearfully but hopefully remained with Jesus to the end were bewildered and in despair. Only their memories now bonded them with their Master, and these were fast being swallowed up by their excruciating hours before the cross. It was a fearful, death-dealing finale. They had expected a great new day for the people of God, but the miracle they had expected had not come. Now it was too late.

THE END AND THE BEGINNING

That might well have been the end of the story. History abounds with visionaries who proposed schemes, died, and were never heard of again. In this case, however, it was just the beginning. Within a short time Jesus's followers were preaching the gospel of their risen Lord.

We do not know exactly what happened after Jesus was entombed. We are told that when on Sunday morning Mary and Martha went to the tomb to mourn, they found the stone that had blocked its entrance rolled away and the tomb empty. The modern ethos dismisses their reports, but we should be careful here, for world-class physicist John Polkinghorne, who in his second career is an Anglican pastor, believes that the tomb really was empty; and New Testament scholars of the stature of N. T. Wright argue that if we take into account all the information available, it points to that conclusion as well, and there is no reason to think that Jesus's body was purloined. As for the stone being rolled away, there is a parallel account in Buddhism where it is said that when the Buddha's closest disciple, Ananda, went to pay reverence to Mahakashyapa at his meditation cave on Vulture Peak, he found that the cave had opened by itself. The stone that had blocked its entrance had been rolled to one side.

In any case, Jesus appears to have been resurrected. Not resuscitated, for his resurrected body differed importantly from the one that died on the cross. It was visible: some people (but not all) recognized it as that of the Jesus they knew. And it was corporeal: the resurrected Jesus hungered and ate, and Thomas touched the spear wound in his side. At the same time, in ways it was incorporeal: it passed through closed doors. These mysterious differences persuaded the disciples that their Master had entered a new mode of being.

In his sonnet "The Resurrection," John Donne wrote, "He was all gold when he lay down, but rose / All tincture." Donne was referring to alchemy, whose ultimate object was not just to turn baser metals into gold, but to discover a tincture that would turn any metal it touched into gold. The risen Christ had become this tincture, turning the lives he touched into "gold." Thenceforth, his people would be Jesus's body, doing what he would do if he still had physical hands and feet.

THE ASCENSION AND PENTECOST

Forty days after he died, Jesus brought his earthly career to a solemn close by ascending into heaven. And forty days after that, God sent the disciples the Comforter Jesus had promised them in an event we now know as Pentecost.

Indissolubly bonded in friendship and sorrow, Jesus's followers had regathered in Jerusalem almost three months after his death to join in the thanksgiving festival in which the first fruits of the harvest were offered to Yahweh. While they were in an upper room, scripture tells us, suddenly from heaven there came a sound like the rush of a violent wind, and it filled the entire home where they were sitting. Divided tongues, as of fire, appeared among them, and a tongue rested on each of them. All of them were filled with the Holy Spirit.

Astonished, the group poured out into the Temple courtyard and found that they could converse in their respective dialects and languages with Jews who had come to Jerusalem from outlying areas for the festivities. This was seen as a portent that Jesus's message would be carried to the ends of the earth.

The expansion began quickly. Empowered by the tongues of fire that had descended on their heads, Jesus's disciples fanned out from Jerusalem, where the persecution against them was severest, into the surrounding Hellenic, Gentile world. Welcoming Gentiles into the community of Christ's followers was a prickly point, but after much internal controversy the move was made, with Peter taking the lead. The disciples started to preach the good news of the risen Christ throughout the region, and burgeoning Christian communities sprang up in its major cities. People found themselves responding to their message, and we must try to understand why.

THE GOOD NEWS

Jesus's resurrection was not about the fate of a worthy man. It concerned the status of goodness in the universe, offering evidence that goodness has power—indeed, ultimate power.

Jesus was goodness incarnate, and in his resurrection his goodness triumphed. If Golgotha had been the end, the goodness Jesus embodied would have been beautiful, yes, but how significant would it have been? A fragile blossom afloat on the world's torrential stream, soon to be drowned—how relevant is goodness if it has no purchase on reality, no power at its disposal? The resurrection reversed the cosmic position in which the cross had placed Jesus's goodness. "Grave, where is your victory? Death, where is your sting?" In James Russell Lowell's rendition in "The Present Crisis":

> Truth forever on the scaffold,
> Wrong forever on the throne,—
> Yet that scaffold sways the future,
> and, behind the dim unknown,
> Standeth God within the shadow,
> keeping watch above his own.

The compassion the disciples had encountered in Jesus was powerful—victorious over everything.

This conviction had transformed a dozen or so disconsolate followers of a slain and discredited leader into one of the most dynamic forces in human history, and the tongues of fire that descended upon them at Pentecost set the Mediterranean world aflame. People who were not speakers waxed eloquent. They exploded across the Greco-Roman world, preaching what has come to be called "the gospel"; in the original Greek the phrase is "the Good News." They spread their message with such fervor that in Jesus's very generation it took root in every major city of the region.

What was this Good News that spawned the Christian church and snapped history into B.C. and A.D. as if it were a dry twig? It wasn't Jesus's ethical teachings; we have already noted that all of those were already in the literature of his day. In fact, it wasn't anything that Jesus taught. Paul, whose letters epitomize the concerns of the early church, was well acquainted with what Jesus had taught, but he almost never referred to those teachings. It wasn't even the way Jesus had embodied his teachings in his life that was the Good News.

What it was can be approached by way of a symbol. If we had been living around the eastern Mediterranean in the early centuries of the Christian era, we might have noticed, scratched here and there on the sides of walls and houses or simply on the ground, the crude outline of a fish. Even if we had seen one of these, we would probably have dismissed it as innocuous graffiti, for these were mainly seaport towns where fishing was a part of daily life. Had we been Christians, however, we would have recognized these drawings as the logo for the Good News. The heads of these fishes would have pointed us toward the places where local Christian groups held their clandestine meetings—underground (in catacombs) or in the back rooms of shops and homes, because to be known as a Christian was to risk the danger of being thrown to lions or gladiators, or turned into a human torch. A cross would have been a giveaway symbol, so a fish substituted for it, for the Greek letters for the word "fish" are also the first letters of the Greek words for "Jesus Christ, Son of God, Savior."

What does that phrase, "Jesus Christ, Son of God, Savior," mean? Rather than plunging into its immense history we will do better to try to enter into the experience that gave rise to that history.

The people who heard Jesus's disciples proclaiming the Good News were as impressed by what they saw as by what they heard. They saw lives that had been transformed—men and women who were ordinary in every way except for the fact that they seemed to have found the secret of living. They evinced a tranquillity, simplicity, and cheerfulness that their hearers had nowhere else encountered. Here were people who seemed to be making a success of the enterprise everyone would like to succeed at—life itself.

Specifically, there seemed to be two qualities in which their lives abounded. The first of these was mutual regard. One of the earliest observations by an outsider about Christians that we have is, "See how these Christians love one another." Integral to this mutual regard was a total absence of social barriers; it was a discipleship of equals. Here were men and women who not only said that everyone was equal in the sight of God but who lived as though they meant it. The conventional barriers of race, gender, and status meant nothing to them, for in Christ there was neither Jew nor Gentile, male nor female, slave nor free. As a consequence, in spite of differences in function or social position, their fellowship was marked by a sense of genuine equality.

Their second distinctive quality was happiness. When Jesus was in danger, his disciples were alarmed; but otherwise it was impossible to be sad in Jesus's company. And when he told his disciples that he wanted his joy to be in them, "that your joy may be complete," to a remarkable degree that objective was realized.

Outsiders found this baffling. These scattered Christians were not numerous. They were not wealthy or powerful, and they were in constant danger of being killed. Yet they had laid hold of an inner peace that found expression in a joy that was uncontainable. Perhaps "radiant" would be a better word. "Radiance" is hardly the word used to characterize the average religious life, but no other word fits as well the life of these early Christians.

When we come to Paul we find him a vivid example. Here was a man who had been ridiculed, driven from town to town, shipwrecked, imprisoned, flogged until his back was covered with stripes. Yet here was a life in which joy was the constant refrain: "Joy unspeakable and full of glory." "Thanks be to God who gives us the victory." "In all things we are more than conquerors." "God who commanded the light to shine out of darkness has shined in our hearts." "Thanks be to God for his unspeakable gift." The joy of these early Christians *was* unspeakable. As the fifth chapter of Ephesians suggests, they sang, not routinely but from the irrepressible overflow of their direct experience. Life was not challenges to be met; it was glory discerned.

What produced this love and joy in these early Christians? Everyone wants those qualities; the question is how to get them. The explanation, insofar as we are able to gather from the New Testament record, is that three intolerable burdens had suddenly and dramatically been lifted from believer's shoulders.

The first of these was fear, including the fear of death. We have it from Swiss psychologist Carl Jung that he never met a patient over forty whose problems did not root back to the fear of approaching death. The reason the Christians could not be intimidated by the lions (and even sang as they entered the coliseum) was that Jesus's counsel, "Fear not, for I am with you," had gotten through to them.

The second burden they had been released from was guilt. Recognized or repressed, guilt seems built into the human condition, for no one lives up to his or her ideals completely. It is not only that we behave less well toward others than our conscience dictates; we also fail ourselves by leaving talents undeveloped and letting opportunities slip by. As a result, we have a hard time living with ourselves. We may manage to keep remorse at bay while the sun is up, but in the sleepless hours of the night it comes through and we feel

> . . . the rending pain of re-enactment
> Of all that you have done, and been; the shame
> Of motives late revealed, and the awareness
> Of things ill done and done to others' harm
> Which once you took as exercise of virtue.
> T. S. Eliot, "Little Gidding"

Oppressive guilt reduces creativity. In its acute form it can rise to a fury of self-condemnation that shuts life down. Paul had felt its force before he was released: "Wretched man that I am! Who will rescue me from this body of death?"

The third release the early Christians experienced was from the cramping confines of the ego. There is no reason to suppose that prior to their new life these men and women were more self-centered than the next person, but they knew that their love was radically confined. They knew that the human curse is to love and sometimes to love well, but never to love *well enough*. Now that curse had been dramatically lifted.

It is not difficult to see how release from fear, guilt, and self-centeredness could feel like rebirth. If someone were to free us from these crippling impediments, we too would call that person Savior. But this only pushes our question back a step. How did the Christians get free of these burdens? And what did a man named Jesus, now gone, have to do with the process, that they should credit it as his doing?

The only power that can effect transformations of the order we have described is love. It remained for the twentieth century to discover that locked within the atom is the energy of the sun itself. For this energy to be released, however, the atom must be bombarded from without. So too, locked in every human being is a store of love that partakes of the Divine —the *imago Dei*, the image of God that is within us. And it too can be activated only through bombardment—in its case, love's bombardment. The process begins in infancy, when a mother's initially unilateral loving smile awakens love in her baby and, as the infant's coordination develops, elicits the flickerings of its answering smile. The process continues into childhood. A loving human being is not produced by exhortations, rules, and threats. Love takes root in children only when it comes to them. (When the activist folk singer Pete Seeger was asked by an interviewer for advice as to how to raise children, he said, "Pour in the love and it will come out from them.") Love is an answering phenomenon. It is, literally, a re-sponse.

An actual incident may help to bring this point home:

A young man was a diffident freshman in a small midwestern college when one morning the instructor (who was his role model and whom he idolized) opened the class by saying, "Last evening as I was reading the papers you recently turned in, I came upon several of the most significant sentences that I can recall ever having read." As the instructor proceeded to read those sentences aloud, the student could hardly believe his ears. His heart leaped into his throat, for he was hearing his own words being read back to him! As he recorded the incident in his journal:

> I don't remember another thing that occurred during that hour, but I shall never forget my feelings when the bell brought me back to my senses. It was noon, and when I stepped outdoors October was never so beautiful. If anyone had asked me for anything, maybe even to lay down my life, I would have given it gladly, for I wanted nothing for myself. I ached only to give to a world that had given so much to me.

If a young man found himself thus changed by the interest a human being had shown in him, perhaps we can understand the way the early Christians were changed by feeling certain that they were totally loved—not abstractly or in principle but vividly and personally—by one who united all power and all goodness. If we too felt loved this way, the experience could dissolve fear, guilt, and self-concern dramatically. As Kierkegaard noted, if at every moment both present and future we were certain that nothing has happened or could ever happen that would separate us from the infinite love of the Infinite, that would be the clearest reason there is for joy.

God's love is precisely what the first Christians did feel. They had experienced Jesus's love and had become convinced that Jesus was God incarnate. Once that love reached them, it could not be stopped. Melting the barriers of fear, guilt, and self-centeredness, it poured through them like a torrential stream, heightening the love they had hitherto felt for others to the point where the difference in *degree* became a difference in *kind*. A new quality, Christian love, was born. Conventional love is evoked by lovable qualities in the beloved, but the love that people encountered from Christ embraced sinners and outcasts, Samaritans and enemies. It gave, not prudentially in order to receive, but because giving was its nature. Paul's famous description of Christian love in the thirteenth chapter of First Corinthians ought not to be read as if he were describing a quality that was already known. His words list the attributes of a specific person, Jesus Christ. In phrases of unparalleled beauty, it describes the divine love that Paul believed Christians would reflect toward others once they experienced Christ's love for them. The reader should approach Paul's words in the understanding that they define a novel capacity that, as it had been fully realized "in the flesh" only in Christ, Paul was describing for the first time:

Love is patient; love is kind; love is not envious or boastful or arrogant or rude. It does not insist on its own way; it is not irritable or resentful; it does not rejoice in wrongdoing, but rejoices in the truth. Love bears all things, believes all things, hopes all things, endures all things. Love never ends.

So astonishing did the first Christians find this love, and the fact that it had actually entered their lives, that they had to appeal for help in describing it. In closing one of the earliest recorded sermons on the Good News, Paul turned back to the words of one of the prophets, who in turn was speaking for God: "Look at this, you scornful souls, and lose yourselves in wonder; for in your days I do such a deed that, if men were to tell you this story, you would not believe it."

THE MYSTICAL BODY OF CHRIST

The first Christians who spread the Good News throughout the Mediterranean world did not feel that they were alone. They were not even alone together, for they believed that Jesus was in their midst as a concrete, energizing power. They remembered that he had said, "Where two or three are gathered in my name, I am there among them. So, while their contemporaries were nicknaming them Christ-ians (literally "the Messiah-folk," because they believed Jesus to be the redeemer the prophets had foretold), they began to call themselves an *ekklesia*. In the Greek of their day this meant no more than a self-governing assembly, but for the Christians the assembly was not a self-help society, a merely human association in which people of goodwill banded together to encourage one another in good works and lift themselves by their collective bootstraps. Human members constituted the Christian *ekkle-sia*, but it was powered by Christ's—read God's—presence within it. The English word for this would be "church."

Completely convinced that God was empowering them, the disciples went forth to possess a world they believed God had already given them. Images came to mind to characterize the intense corporate identity they felt. One of these came from Christ himself: "I am the vine, you are the branches." This is obviously a metaphor, but we shall miss its force unless we see the exact sense in which the early church read it. Just as an empowering substance, sap, flows through the vine, entering its branches, leaves, and fruit to bring life to them, so a spiritual substance, the Holy Spirit, was flowing from the resurrected Christ into his followers, empowering them with the love that bore good works as its fruit. This was the way Jesus's followers read his own statement of the matter: "I am the true vine. Abide in me as I abide in you. Just as the branch cannot bear fruit by itself unless it abides in the vine, neither can you unless you abide in me."

Paul adapted Christ's image by using the human body instead of a vine to symbolize the church. This preserved the vine's image of a central life-substance that animated its parts, but at the same time granted the parts more latitude in being free standing. Though the offices and talents of individual Christians might differ as much as eyes and feet, Paul argued, all are animated by a single source. "For as in one body we have many members, so we who are many are one body in Christ."

This seemed to the early Christians to be the completely appropriate image for their corporate life. The church was the Mystical Body of Christ. "Mystical" here meant supernatural and mysterious but not unreal—quite the opposite, in fact. The human form of Christ had left the earth, but he was continuing his uncompleted mission through a new physical body, his church, of which he remained the head. This Mystical Body was born in the "upper room" in Jerusalem at Pentecost through the animating power of the Holy Spirit. For "what the soul is to the body of man," Saint Augustine would later write, "that the Holy Spirit is to the Body of Christ, which is the Church."

If Christ was the head of this body and the Holy Spirit its soul, individual Christians were its cells, few at first but increasing as the body came of age. The cells of an organism are not isolates; they draw their life from the enveloping vitality of their hosts, while at the same time contributing to that vitality. The analogy is exact. The aim of early Christian worship was to say those words and do those things that kept the Mystical Body alive, while at the same time opening individual cells—souls—to its inflowing vitality. The transaction literally "incorporated" Christians into Christ's person, for in an important sense Christ now *was* the church. In any given Christian the divine life might be flowing fully, partially, or not at all, according to whether his or her faith was vital, perfunctory, or apostate, the latter condition being comparable to paralysis. Some cells might even turn cancerous and endanger their host: these are the Christians Paul speaks of as bringing disrepute upon the church by falling into scandal. But to the degree that members were in Christian health, the pulse of the Holy Spirit coursed through them. This bound Christians to one another and at the same time placed them in the closest conceivable relation to Christ himself. "Do you not know that your bodies are members of Christ?" And again, "It is no longer I who live, but it is Christ who lives in me."

Building upon this early conception of the church, Christians over the years have come to think of the church as having a double aspect. Insofar as it consists of Christ and the Holy Spirit dwelling in people and suffusing them with grace and love, it is flawless. Insofar as it consists of fallible human members, it always falls short of its possibility. The worldly face of the church is always open to criticism, which must often be severe. But its mistakes, Christians hold, have been due to its human fabric.

As was noted in Part One of this book, Christians differ on whether there is salvation apart from the Body of Christ. To summarize what was said there:

First, historical circumstances must be taken into consideration when reading categorical withholdings of salvation from outsiders. Who are the outsiders from whom salvation is being withheld? How lofty is their faith, how advanced their moral standards?

Second, even in the first millennium there were differences of opinion on this point. Today, liberal Protestants tend to reject completely the claim that *ex ecclesia nulla solis est,* "outside the church there is no salvation," seeing that claim as religious imperialism. At the other end of the spectrum are fundamentalists who insist that none but those who are knowingly and formally Christians will be saved. In between are those who answer the question by drawing a distinction between the church visible and the church invisible. The church visible is composed of those who are formally members of the church as an earthly institution. Pope Pius IX spoke for the majority of Christians when he rejected the idea that membership in the church visible is indispensable to salvation. Those who abide, he said, by

> the natural law, the commands of which are written by God in every human heart, and being ready to obey him, live honorably and uprightly, can, with the power of Divine light and grace helping them, attain eternal life. For God, who clearly sees, searches out, and knows the minds, hearts, thoughts, and dispositions of all, in his great goodness and mercy does not by any means suffer a man to be punished with eternal torments, who is not guilty of voluntary faults.

This statement allows for those who are not members of the church visible to be saved. Some Christians add to this the belief that the divine life pulses more strongly through the church visible than through any other institution.

SAUL OF TARSUS

It has not been possible to avoid jumping the gun by referring frequently to Paul—he has been lavishly quoted in the preceding pages—but it is now time to turn directly to Saul of Tarsus who at and after his baptism used Paul, his Roman name, to underscore his conversion from Judaism.

If Christ founded Christianity, Paul founded the Christian church. Its seeds had been sown in the analogies of the vine and its branches and the Mystical body of Christ, but Paul gave those understandings institutional shape, a visible structure.

Institutions, organizations of whatsoever sort, have problems built into them; they come with territory. Those problems must be faced and dealt with, for it is institutions that give ideas traction in history. If Jesus had not been followed by Paul, the Sermon on the Mount would have evaporated in a generation or two; but as it is, we still hear and heed it. Comparably, if the Buddha had not instituted the *sangha*—his monastic community—his teachings too would have vanished from the face of the earth.

Paul is in Christians' bones. Two thousand years after his birth, he still affects all parts of their lives: their views on God and Jesus and what they promised and demanded, along with their thoughts and feelings on guilt and innocence, on daily life in this world, and on the rewards and punishments stored up for them in the next. The list goes on and on.

Saul bursts on the scene dramatically. Among the Jews who were determined to stamp out the Christ-heresy that was nibbling around the edges of their religion, none was more zealous than Saul of Tarsus: it was the passion of his life.

One day when Saul was traveling to Damascus with orders from the high priests to bind and bring back to Jerusalem as many Christians as he could lay hold of, suddenly a blinding light, greater than that of the sun, engulfed his company. Saul was knocked to the ground and heard a voice saying, "Saul, Saul, why do you persecute me?" When he asked who was speaking, the voice replied, "I am Jesus, whom you are persecuting." The light left him blind for three days; he had to be led the rest of the way to Damascus, where he managed to locate a Christian household and was baptized.

We need to look closely at this conversion experience. In the way that house lights go down in theaters when the stage lights come up, Saul's ocular blindness sharpened the vision of what was disclosed to his inner, spiritual eye. Being a knowledgeable Jew, Saul recognized what he saw. He, Saul of all people, was heir to the "throne mysticism" of the Jews. Christians are not familiar with the phrase "throne mysticism," but Jews know it well. Its outstanding representatives included Enoch, Ezekiel, and Isaiah, who in the year that King Uzziah died "saw the Lord sitting on a throne, high and lofty," with the hem of his robe filling the entire Temple.

Paul referred to his vision only once, and then only indirectly and under the veil of anonymity. In a letter to the Corinthians he spoke of having been taken to the "third heaven" and shown there things he was forbidden to disclose. Because of that proscription, he could not say that it was Jesus, clothed in dazzling white, that he had seen seated on the throne; but it is reasonable to infer that it was, for nothing short of an overwhelming revelation of this magnitude could account for the instantaneousness of his conversion and the force with which it catapulted him onto the stage of history.

Paul seems to have been providentially endowed for his new mission. He was zealous—as zealous in converting people to Christianity as he had been in persecuting them. He was energetic, crisscrossing the Mediterranean world tirelessly. (When in a vision he saw a man in Macedonia, the stepping-stone to

Europe, pleading, "Come over to Macedonia and help us," he and Timothy went.) His dedication to eliminating social barriers came straight from Jesus and wrung from him one of his most forceful pronouncements: "There is neither Jew nor Greek, there is neither slave nor free, there is neither male nor female, for you are all one in Christ Jesus." Paul was not a spellbinding evangelist, but guided by the Holy Spirit he knew what might be profanely called the tricks of the trade, and when he infused these with the intensity of his conviction, he was persuasive. He was a brilliant commander, rallying his troops and keeping them in line. He was a skilled administrator, revisiting his churches as often as he could, and when he couldn't, sending his inquiries and directives through messengers. He would listen, praise, explain, reason, or cajole as the case required, but if things came to a showdown, he would lay down the law.

Out of all this, and doubling back to inform it, there emerged a theology that was so original and impressive that St. Augustine and Martin Luther (to cite only the two most famous cases) credited him with shaping their own understandings.

That theology emerged from Paul's personal experience. As already noted, it was a bitter experience ("wretched man that I am"), because it convinced him that it was impossible for him to obtain the peace and joy he needed with his own feeble resources—in a word, he could not save himself. That is the realization which (on the other side of the world) split Buddhism into Theravada and Mahayana, and (at the other end of history) caused Bill Wilson to found Alcoholics Anonymous. We are back to the point that has already been made: only something—love—that bombards the ego from without can crack its hard shell. The issue came to be encapsulated in a disjunction, faith versus works, with Pauline theology siding with faith. An undernoticed feature of William James's classic *The Varieties of Religious Experience* is his argument (quiet, to be sure) that those who are "twice-born" understand religion more profoundly than do the "once-born," for (as was the case with William James himself, who waged a lifelong battle with depression) they experience more powerfully what the unsaved life *is*.

We have spoken of Paul's manifold endowments, but one remains to be mentioned. He was a poet, and a great one. His words are so filled with energy, so charged with grievous force, that he seems to have been incapable of composing a prosaic sentence. His discourses sift out the superfluous without omitting anything of importance; they help us to comprehend the incomprehensible; and they exude intelligence and ecstasy combined—as if that delivery were as easy as breathing. Without intelligence he would have perished in duels with one or another of the church's opponents, who certainly didn't lack for dialectical ability, and without ecstasy his words would not have reached their distinctive heights and would have remained simply good poetry.

All of these virtues came together to cause Paul's sayings to permeate the thoughts of Christians almost as much as the sayings of Jesus. Samples have laced the preceding pages, but others (with a few repetitions) are worth drawing together here, to bring to our concerted attention his poetic powers.

Beholding the glory of the Lord, we are ourselves transformed from glory into glory.

Whatsoever is true, whatsoever is honorable, whatsoever is just, whatsoever is pure, whatsoever is pleasing, whatsoever is commendable, if there is any excellence and if there is anything worthy of praise, think about these things.

Don't let the present press you into its mold. Instead, be transformed by the renewing of your minds.

In all things we are more than conquerors through him who loved us. For I am persuaded that neither death, nor life, nor angels, nor rulers, nor things present, nor things to come, nor powers, nor height, nor depth, nor anything else in all creation will be able to separate us from the love of God in Christ Jesus our Lord.

I have learned in every circumstance wherein I find myself, therein to be content, for we know that all things work together for good for those who love God.

Let us not fall asleep as others do, but let us keep awake and be sober. For those who sleep, sleep at night, and those who get drunk get drunk at night. But since we belong to the day, let us be sober and put on the breastplate of faith and love, and the hope of salvation as our helmet.

When I was a child I spoke like a child, I thought like a child, I reasoned like a child. But now that I am a man, I have given up childish things.

We who are in this earthly tent are groaning under its weight. But we do not want to be relieved of it; we want to expand it until our mortality phases into immortality. It is God who effects that change, the God who has given us as down payment his Holy Spirit.

His masterpiece, though, was his already quoted but worth-repeating description of love, which innumerable Christians know by heart:

If I speak with the tongues of men and of angels, but have not love, I am as clanking brass and tinkling cymbal. And if I have prophetic powers, and knowledge, and if I have faith to remove mountains but do not have love, I am nothing. If I give away all my possessions and hand over my body so that I may boast but do not have love, I gain nothing.

Love is patient; love is kind; love is not envious or boastful or arrogant or rude. It does not insist on having its own way; it is not irritable or resentful; it does not rejoice in wrongdoing, but it rejoices in the truth. Love bears all things, believes all things, hopes all things, endures all things. Love never ends. Now abideth faith, hope, and love, and the greatest of these is love.

This section on Paul concludes our account of the Jesus that the New Testament gives us, and we should take note of the fact—so important that it will be repeated a number of times in this book—that truth is the *whole*. We miss the truth if we content ourselves with fragments.

The Gospels give us a good example of this in providing four accounts of Jesus that complement one another in the way four people's memories of a departed friend provide a more rounded view of him than a single reminiscence could. On the issue of origins, Matthew traces Jesus's lineage back to Abraham, and in doing so tells us in effect that we cannot understand Jesus unless we recognize that he was a dyed-in-the-wool Jew. Mark adds: to be sure, but at the same time we cannot understand Jesus unless we see how uniquely he played out his Jewishness; so Mark bypasses lineage altogether and opens his account with Jesus's baptism. Then comes Luke to throw a priestly mantle over Jesus's individuality by opening his account with the angel Gabriel's visit to the priest Zechariah while the latter was performing his office in the Holy of Holies. Luke tells how Gabriel announced that Elizabeth, the priest's wife, would give birth to the John who would launch Jesus's ministry by baptizing him. Finally there is John, who—without denying any of the above—tells us that we cannot possibly understand Jesus if we omit his cosmic stature and station: "In the beginning was the Word [*Logos,* a Greek word which Christians used to refer to Christ] and the Word was God. All things came into being through him, and without him not one thing came into being." This compact formula compresses everything into Christ. He is the world's beginning and its end. He is the vessel into which God pours himself completely and descends to the lowest depths of creation, where he gathers everything back into himself and fulfills it at the end of time. It takes all four Gospels to tell us who / what Jesus in his fullness was and is.

THE MIND OF THE CHURCH

It was not the disciples' *minds* that were first drawn to Jesus. Rather, as we have seen, it was their *experience*—the experience of living in the presence of someone whose selfless love, crystalline joy, and preternatural power came together in a way his disciples found divinely mysterious. It was only a matter of time, however, before Christians felt the need to understand this experience in order to explain it to themselves and to others; its mystery would remain, but if their intelligence was rightly deployed, it could help them to enter the experience more deeply. Christian theology was born, and from then on the church was head as well as heart. Secularism has put theology on the defensive, however, so before we examine the content of Christian theology we must argue the importance of that discipline itself.

People today are more interested in psychology and ethics than in theology and metaphysics; people resonate more to the Sermon on the Mount than to the theological arguments of St. Paul, St. Augustine, and St. Thomas Aquinas. This is understandable, but it doesn't alter the fact that to reduce religion to psychology and ethics is to denature it. "Are moderns really better off with the theories of psychology than with the hard thoughts of Jeremiah or Jesus?" Harvard psychiatrist Robert Coles asks rhetorically. Religion must include the summons to the upright life, but its eyes are not fixed primarily on that summons. Faith's focal attention is on a vision of reality that sets morality in motion, as a byproduct almost.

Religion begins with experience—ritual, belief, and experience, and (to echo the cadence of St. Paul's aphorism) the greatest of these is experience. The experience of things that inspire us gives rise to symbols as the mind tries to think about these invisible, inspiring things. Symbols are ambiguous, however, so eventually the mind introduces thoughts to resolve the ambiguities of symbols and to systematize intuitions. Reading this sequence backward we can define theology as the systematization of thoughts about the symbols that religious experience gives rise to. What follows is an account of the foundational points in Christian theology: the incarnation, the atonement, the trinity, life everlasting, the resurrection of the body, hell, and the virgin birth.

The Incarnation

Among the revealed religions, Christianity is unique in not being content merely to juxtapose the Absolute and the contingent, the Divine and the human; it conjoins them from the start. For the prologue in the book of John reads: "In the beginning was the Word ... and the Word was God." Thus the mystery of the incarnation (and the redemption which it entails) is built into Christianity from the start. It took several centuries, however, for the church to become consciously aware of and describe the framework of this mystery.

The doctrine of the incarnation affirms that Christ was God-man; simultaneously both fully God and fully man. To say that such a contention is paradoxical seems like a charitable way of putting the matter. It looks more like a blatant contradiction. If the doctrine held that Christ was half human and half divine, or that he was divine in certain respects while being human in others, our minds would not balk. But such concessions are precisely what the church's creeds—formulations of canonical beliefs recited in worship services—refuse to grant. In the words of the Creed of Chalcedon, hammered out in the fifth century, Jesus Christ was "at once complete in Godhead and complete in manhood, truly God and truly man, of one essence with the Father as regards his Godhead, and at the same time of one essence with us as regards his manhood, in all respects like us, apart from sin."

The church has always admitted that such assertions are opaque, but it refuses to let that be the last word on the matter. Actually, science takes the same position. The anomalies of frontier physics provoked J. B. S. Haldane to his famous "mutterance" that "the universe is not only queerer than we suppose, but queerer than we *can* suppose;" and it is commonly said that the only problem with quantum mechanics (which has been tested for accuracy to twelve decimal places) is that it violates common sense; it is counterintuitive. In more than one field, it appears, reality can be too strange for logic to map, and when logic and evidence clash, it is prudent to stick with evidence, for this holds the prospect of leading to a wider logic, whereas the opposite approach closes the door to discovery.

In suggesting that it was evidence that forced Christians to their logic-taxing assertion that Christ was both human and divine, we are of course speaking of the evidence of religious experience—intuitions of the soul concerning ultimate issues of existence. Such evidence cannot be presented with an obviousness that compels assent, for it does not turn on sense reports. But if we try, we can have an intimation at least of the experiential leads that the Christians were following.

There is no way of understanding the creeds without seeing them against the Mediterranean background in which they were set. We can begin with the gods that peopled that world: the Olympian deities were human beings writ large, sharing their foibles on a grand scale. Obviously the Christians' God didn't fit that mold, and the early church's doctrine of the incarnation made that clear.

The earliest creed is the Apostles' Creed, which gets its name from the (unverifiable) supposition that Jesus's disciples set it in place. Because its theme was the God-man splice, it had of course to address both of its poles, but the way it did so is surprising. Flying as it does in the face of logic, it was an affront both then and now, but in different ways. What we find hard to believe today is that Jesus was divine, whereas in the Greco-Roman world it was his humanity that had to be argued for.

When in the year 325 the Emperor Constantine convened the Council of Nicaea to decide whether Christ was of the same substance as God or only of *like* substance, three hundred bishops and their attendants came rushing in a frenzy of excitement from all over the empire. They must have presented a strange sight, for many of them bore empty eye sockets, disfigured faces, and limbs that were twisted and paralyzed from the Diocletian persecution they had endured. Obviously, more than forensics was involved in the deliberations of these men. This was not just an ecclesiastical debating contest.

The Nicene decision that Christ was "of one substance with the Father" claimed something about both Jesus and God. Note first what it claimed about Jesus:

Among the many possible meanings the word "God" carries, none is more important than "that to which one should give oneself without reservation." In saying that Jesus was God, one of the things the church was saying was that his life provides the perfect model for that self-giving—in other words, the perfect model for the way human beings should order their lives. Slavish imitation of details is never creative, but insofar as Christ's love, his freedom, and the daily beauty of his life can find their authentic parallels in our own, we are carried Godward, for the traits are authentically divine.

This much is obvious. But as we enter more deeply into the doctrine of the incarnation, we must be prepared for surprises.

As noted above, though the Christian announcement of the incarnation—of a God-man—was as startling in its day as it is in ours, the shock attaches to different poles. Because we find disturbing the thought that a human being can be divine, we find the shocking feature of the incarnation to be what it says about Jesus: that he was God. But in its own world, where the dividing line between the human and the Divine was perforated to the point that even emperors routinely claimed to be divine, a struggling sect's claim that its founder was divine raised few eyebrows. "So what else is new?" would have been the common, dismissive response.

The incarnation claimed that there was something new in the Christian message; namely, its proclamation of the *kind* of God that God was, as demonstrated by God's willingness to assume a human form and live a human life. That willingness, together with the character of Jesus's life added up to a differ-ent—indeed, radical—understanding of divinity that shocked the Mediterranean world and set it on its heels. In this upstart view, God was *concerned* about humanity; concerned enough to suffer in its behalf. This was unheard of, to the point that the reaction to it was disbelief followed by alarm. In the eyes of threatened conservatives, such blasphemy, coupled with the Christians' radically egalitarian social views, justified per-secution to stamp out this new sect, and Christians were forced into catacombs. That Christians were aware of the nov-elty of their theology is illustrated by the fact that they seldom referred to God without stipulating that it was "the God and Father of our Lord Jesus Christ" that they were talking about.

As for what the doctrine of the incarnation asserts about Christ, here too it shocked the Mediterranean world. For in-stead of wasting many words on Jesus's divinity, the Apostles Creed argued for his full humanity. (Later, when Arius ap-peared on the scene, arguing that Jesus's substance was similar but subordinate to God's, this imbalance needed to be cor-rected and the Nicene Creed did that and Arianism was pro-nounced heretical.) But here we are concerned with the Apostles' Creed, the relevant portion of which reads:

> I believe in God the Father almighty, Maker of heaven and earth, and in Jesus Christ our Lord, who was *con-ceived* by the Holy Ghost, *born* of the Virgin Mary, *suffered* under Pontius Pilate, was *crucified, died,* and *buried. . . .*

How casually this touches on Christ's divinity—which as we have seen didn't need to be argued for at that time—and how hard it comes down on his humanity. He really was *born,* it says; he really *suffered,* he really *died* and was *buried.* These events were not just make-believe, a sequence through which God merely seemed to brush with the human estate. Christ endured these experiences as fully as we do. He was "truly man."

It is not difficult to see why (even at the cost of immense logical awkwardness) the church felt that it needed to retain Christ's humanity. A bridge must touch both banks, and Christ was the bridge that joined humanity to God—"God became man that man might become God," was Bishop Irenaeus's way of putting the matter. Jesus Christ, indisputably divine, had also to be through-and-through human, right down to the biological, cellular level, if his divinity was to infuse our humanity. The Christians could have relaxed one claim or the other and salvaged logic, but only at the cost of betraying the imperative of the incarnation.

The Atonement

Turning now to the doctrine of the atonement, the centerpiece of Christianity, we learn that its root meaning is *reconciliation,* the recovery of the wholeness that at-one-ment points toward. Early Christians were convinced that Christ's death had effected an unparalleled rapprochement between God and humanity to counter the tragic estrangement between the two that had occurred—somehow it had put them right with God. They saw the words of the prophet Isaiah—"He was wounded for our transgressions; by his stripes we are healed of our transgressions" as anticipating the words of St. Paul: "In Christ God was reconciling the world to himself."

How is this to be understood? To answer that question we need to reintroduce something that was said in Part One of this book, collapsing it here into three points:

- Because there is no commensurability between the Infinite and the finite, the human mind cannot comprehend exactly what happens in God's dealings with humanity. This precludes our knowing exactly *how* Christ's death on the cross accomplished the reconciliation between man and God.

- To try to understand what happened, we need a *formula*. Here again science points the way. Scientists suggest that if we want to understand what an atom is, we might visualize its electrons as tennis balls circling around a center, the atom's nucleus. As a heuristic device—a teaching tool—that picture is as good as any, but it would be a mistake to think that an atom is really like that. In the present case, the formula for the atonement is, "God was in Christ reconciling the world unto himself."

- Formulas need to be interpreted. Their interpretations are manifold—almost every major theologian has tried his or her hand at interpreting reconciliation, and these interpretations resemble angles from which a building can be seen. One interpretation that enjoyed considerable vogue, especially in the early centuries of the church, is legalistic. By voluntarily disobeying God's order not to eat of the forbidden fruit in Eden, Adam sinned. As his sin was directed against God, it was of infinite proportion. Sins must be compensated for; otherwise, God's justice would be compromised. An infinite sin demands infinite recompense, and this could be effected only by an Infinite Being, God, vicariously assuming our guilt and paying the ultimate penalty it required, namely, death. God made this payment through the person of Christ, and the debt is canceled.

When the mind of the church had a different cast, this understanding of the atonement carried weight, though Augustine, in the early fifth century, came to believe that its view of a vengeful God was unworthy of the heavenly Father and thus he abandoned this "ransom" theory of Christ's death. In any case, that theory cries out for other interpretations, and we will enter one that stands close to the one Abelard, a French philosopher and theologian, put forward a millennium after Christ.

Our theory begins at the beginning. God created human beings unblemished, as the Garden of Eden story relates. Somewhere down the line, however, a breach occurred that sundered human beings from God. Sin is usually said to be the cause of the breach, and that is not wrong; but a recent Orthodox theologian, Philip Sherrard, puts the issue in a broader perspective that is worth quoting at some length:

The fall may best be understood not as a moral deviation or as a descent into a carnal state, but as a drama of knowledge, as a dislocation and degradation of our consciousness, a lapse of our perceptive and cognitive powers—a lapse which cuts us off from the presence and awareness of other superior worlds and imprisons us in the fatality of our solitary existence in this world. It is to forget the symbolic function of every form and to see in things not their dual, symbolic reality, but simply their non-spiritual dimension, their psycho-physical or material appearance.

Our crime, prolonging that of Adam, is losing the sense of symbols; for to lose the sense of symbols is to be put in the presence of our own darkness, of our own ignorance. This is the exile from Paradise, the condition of our fallen humanity; and it is the consequence of our ambition to establish our presence exclusively in this terrestrial world and to assert that our presence in this world, and exclusively in this world, accords with our real nature as human beings. In fact, we have reached the point not only of thinking that the world which we perceive with our ego-consciousness is the natural world, but also of thinking that our fallen, sub-human state is the natural *human* state, the state that accords with our nature as human beings. And we talk of acquiring knowledge of the natural world when we do not even know what goes on in the mind of an acorn.

This dislocation of our consciousness which defines the fall is perhaps most clearly evident in the divorce we make between the spiritual world and the material, the uncreated and the created, and in our assumption that we can know the one without knowing the other. If we acknowledge the spiritual realm at all, we tend to regard it as something quite other than the material realm and to deny that the Divine is inalienably present in natural forms or can be known except through a direct perception which bypasses the natural world—as though the existence of this world were, spiritually speaking, negative and of no consequence where our salvation is concerned.

What occasioned this dislocation—or better, *who* occasioned it?—for in the biblical world evil is not an abstract concept. It is a person who entered the Garden of Eden disguised as a serpent, a snake in the grass. He has a number of names—Beelzebub, Satan, and Devil are among the best known—and titles such as Prince of Darkness, Ruler of This World, and the Adversary. In the desert following Jesus's baptism, Satan tempted Jesus to turn stones into bread, to display his supernatural powers by jumping off the roof of the Temple, and to inherit the splendors of the world by worshipping him. Jesus had to struggle fiercely to master those temptations, which shows that Satan has great power. How did he come by it?

Evil is a capacity, and capacities mount on the ladder of life. A cow is simply a cow; moral criteria don't apply. One dog can be better or worse behaved than others. A child can be kindhearted or mean-spirited, but it takes an adult to plot and effect evil. Now: Satan was an angel, and even after his fall retained the powers appertaining to angels. Free will is one of these powers, and Satan abused his by trying to usurp God's place, and he became thereby the Fallen Angel. His project was doomed from the start and in principle, because replacing

God is a logical impossibility. But he came close, for though morally flawed he was at the top of the angelic heap and had enormous power. So he became second in command, so to speak—the Prince of Darkness. Beginning by disguising himself as a serpent in the Garden of Eden, he led mankind—and history and nature too—out of the Garden and closed its gates behind them. That's where things stand now, in "outer darkness" and under the "principalities and powers" that Paul railed against so vehemently. That's where they will remain until the end of time. There can never be a smooth synthesis between Christ and culture, because under Satan's spell culture is always "eccentric" in the precise meaning of that word—off-center—and behaves like a shopping cart when it is pushed from the wrong end. Christians live in occupied territory, the territory that served as the landing pad for the incarnation. Another term for this pad is the "established order," for which Kierkegaard reserved his most scathing satire. Asking if it could assure his eternal salvation, he lets the establishment answer for itself:

> Why certainly. And if in the end you encounter some obstacle, be assured that when your last hour comes you will be well baled and crated in one of the large shipments which the established order sends straight through to heaven under its own seal and plainly addressed to "The Eternal Blessedness." You can be assured that you will be exactly as well received and just as blessed as all of the others who are admitted. In short, the established order vouches categorically for your blessedness in the hereafter.

Once Satan landed and staked out his occupied territory, what did God do? Being omnipotent he could have defeated Satan and his forces with a stroke of the pen, so to speak, just as at the beginning he could have wiped Satan off the map the moment he rebelled. But this was not an option for God, for (as has been previously noted) that would have required keeping existence to himself—hoarding it, so to speak. And because there cannot be two Gods, that meant creating an imperfect world and giving it its rein. So, because God could not compel Satan and his subjects to surrender, the only option left to him was to *persuade* those subjects to give up sinning and turn to the good. Persuade them to repent, which doesn't mean simply to feel sorry: it requires backing up—full speed astern—and reversing the human tendency to go one's own way.

How could God do this? The story of a twentieth-century Zen monk points the direction.

The monk lived as a recluse in a hut on the side of a mountain. His only possessions were his robe, his straw sandals, and the bowl with which he begged for his food in the nearby village. The only surviving haiku that he wrote provides an indication of his freedom from attachments, a trait that was one of the reasons the villagers revered him. The evening after a thief stole his sandals and bowl he wrote, "The moon still shines/in my window. Unstolen/by the thief."

One day, as the monk was on his daily food-accepting walk a mother invited him into her home to share the noonday meal with her and her son, whom (she explained before they entered the house) she hoped the monk could straighten out, for the lad was a delinquent and was clearly headed for trouble.

When the son was called to the table he barely acknowledged the monk's presence and stared sullenly at the table throughout the meal. The monk too remained silent as they all ate. But as the monk was preparing to leave, the son did deign to do his duty and tie the monk's straw sandals. As he stooped to do this, he felt a drop of warm water fall on his head. Looking up, he saw tears streaming down the monk's face. The monk's compassion for what was in store for the young man turned the delinquent around, and he mended his ways.

This true story offers a beautiful example of the "power made perfect in weakness" that St. Paul extolled, and it sets the right tone for the interpretation of the atonement I am attempting to give. Apart from God, who *is* love, love is (as has been noted) a response to incoming love, and the most powerful demonstration of the sender's love is to let its receiver know that the sender suffers the pain the recipient suffers—in God's case infinitely, for there is nothing halfway about God. So God incarnated himself, assuming a human aspect in which he could and would suffer. Incarnated, he voluntarily endured the most agonizing death known in his day, in order to break through each recipient's shell and let people know that they are loved. Actually, though, God's agony began with his stuffing his infinity into the tiny duffel bag of a human being (if we may stoop to such an undignified analogy), and thereon hangs a personal anecdote.

I served for a semester as visiting professor at Villanova University. Because it is Roman Catholic, I decided to "do in Rome as the Romans do" and attend Sunday morning masses at a Catholic church a few blocks from my apartment. However, that congregation's liturgy turned out to be innovative beyond my capacity to appreciate, so the following Sunday I checked out a high-church Anglican congregation in the vicinity. I searched no further.

Now it happened that I had to have a hernia operation in the course of the semester—this was back in the days when the operation was more of a production than laser surgery has made it today—and having been instructed to hasten my recovery by keeping as active as I could, I took the cane I had been given and walked the three blocks to the church. I experienced the distance as considerably longer that Sunday than on previous Sundays, and when I reached my pew I was in considerable discomfort. That put me in a good position to take in that morning's sermon, which was titled "The Horror of the Incarnation." The rector asked the congregation to try to imagine the horror that awaited the Godhead when it was forced to cram its infinity into the straitjacket of a mortal frame with its innumerable problems, physical and emotional. I feel confident that on that Sunday morning I was the best person in the congregation to take in experientially what the rector said.

All of this adds up to why the cross is the central symbol of Christianity. The overt symbolism of a cross is so obvious—its vertical arm uniting heaven and earth, and its horizontal arm symbolizing throwing one's arms out to others—that it comes close to being a universal symbol. But wherever throughout the world we see a cross atop a building, we know that we are in the presence of a Christian church. How have Christians plumbed the depths of the cross to make it distinctively *their* signature? Let's try to understand.

It is common knowledge that Jesus spoke seven "words" while he was on the cross:

- To the men who persuaded Pilate to have Jesus crucified: "Father, forgive them for they do not know what they are doing."

- To the thief hanging on the cross beside him who admitted that he was guilty but told the thief on Jesus's other side that the man hanging between them was innocent, "This day you will be with me in paradise."

- In commending his beloved disciple John to his mother who was weeping at the foot of his cross, "Woman, here is your son."

- "My God, why have your forsaken me?"

- "I am thirsty."

- "It is finished."

- "Into your hands I commend my spirit."

Powerful and compelling as those words are, they are not the last word. For the word *of* the cross is more eloquent and compelling than the words Jesus spoke *from* the cross. If we try to articulate what the cross itself says, it is something like this:

Still your tongue. Close your lips. In blunt parlance, shut up. Shut up and simply look. And as you look, remember that the agony I experienced during the three hours that I hung there was for your sake, to heal your transgressions.

Is there anything more that I could have done to demonstrate how much I love you? If this doesn't get through to you, there is nothing more I can do to make my point.

Anne Lamott puts this matter colloquially. To any conceivable complaint we can raise, Jesus says, "O yeah. Me too."

The church fathers were clearly aware that the word of the cross was the most eloquent, not only that God ever spoke but that God *could* speak, which is why they equated Christ crucified with the Good News. In the words of a familiar hymn:

When I survey the wondrous cross
On which the Prince of Glory died,
My greatest gain I count but loss
And pour contempt on all my pride.

Ignatius of Antioch, one of the earliest church fathers, anticipated that hymn by asserting, simply, "My desire has been crucified."

Finally, the word of the cross is not uttered in the past tense. Every time we abuse the poor, every time we pollute our God-given planet, indeed every time we act selfishly, God dies naked on the cross of our ego. Recently a woman was overheard telling her friend that when she looked out at the world she could hardly believe the appalling state it's in. But then she sighed and added softly, as if to herself, "I feel so sorry for God. Poor God."

Does the point of Christ's suffering get through to people? To some, yes; to others, it does not. Christianity would not have come into being if it hadn't gotten through to St. Paul and the Jesus people, who went about preaching the paradoxical message that Christ crucified *was* the Good News. And it gets through today to Christians who see the church as the family of those who have heard the word of the cross and continue to heed it.

The Trinity

The next key Christian doctrine that we shall consider is the Trinity. It holds that while God is fully one, God is also three. The latter half of this claim leads Jews and Muslims to wonder if Christians are truly monotheists, but Christians are confident that they are. H_2O can be ice, water, or steam without losing its chemical identity.

What prompted the early Christians to adopt this atypical view that God is three-in-one? As always in such matters, the idea was anchored in experience and gave voice to it. It was not until the fourth century that that voice was set definitively in place, but the experiences that prompted it began in the early church. Indeed, those experiences *generated* the church. How?

As full-fledged Jews, Jesus's disciples affirmed Yahweh unquestioningly. But as we have seen, they came to see Jesus as

Yahweh's assumption of a human form to enter the world corporeally. And then came Pentecost, which brought the Holy Spirit to the disciples' awareness.

This is how the disciples were brought to their understanding of God in three persons; but once that understanding was in place, they projected it back to the beginning of time. If the divine "triangle" has three "sides" now, they reasoned, it must *always* have had three sides. The Son and the Holy Spirit had proceeded principally from the Father, but not temporally. The three were together from the start; for after the multiplicity in the divine nature was brought home to them, Christians could no longer think of God as complete without it.

We have noted that the other two Abrahamic religions object to this theology, but Christians are committed to it. For love is a relationship, and thus love needs others to bestow it on. If, then, love is not just one of God's attributes but his very essence—and it may be Christianity's distinctive mission in history to claim just that—at no point could God have been truly God without being involved in relationship. That requirement was met "before the foundation of the world" was laid, Paul told the Ephesians. We have already quoted John's assertion that the Word (that is, Jesus) was with God in the beginning and in eternity relationships are logical, not sequential, for time does not touch eternity. And it echoes throughout the corridors of Christian history, as in John Tauler's assertion that "the Father begets the Son in Eternity"—Tauler was a Dominican preacher who is revered for his tireless work among the sick and dying during the Black Death. The Godhead is a society of three divine persons, knowing and loving each other so entirely that not merely can none exist without the others, but in some mysterious way each *is* what the others are. Thus the Nicene Creed affirms,

> We believe in one God the Father almighty, and in one Lord Jesus Christ, the only-begotten Son of God, . . . and in the Holy Spirit, the Lord, the life-giver, who with the Father and the Son together is worshipped and glorified.

In the final section of the *Divine Comedy*, Dante puts the three-in-one thesis poetically:

> *That light supreme, within its fathomless*
> *Clear substance, showed to me three spheres, which bare*
> *Three hues distinct, and occupied one space.*
>
> *The first mirrored the next, as though it were*
> *Rainbow from rainbow, and the third seemed flame*
> *Breathed equally from each of the first pair.*

St. Velimirovich put the point almost as poetically:

> Within me the three Hypostases open at the same time. There is no Father without the Son and no Son without the Holy Spirit. When I lie beside my Lake Ochrid and sleep unconsciously, neither consciousness, nor desire, nor action dies within me—rather they all flow into one blessed, nirvana-like, indistinguishable unity. When the sun pours out its gold over the lake, I awaken not as a

nirvana-like unity, but as a tri-unity of consciousness, desire, and action. This is your history in my soul, O Lord, interpreter of my life.

I will end this discussion of the Trinity on a personal note. It was my great good fortune to have Czeslaw Milosz, one of the great poets of our time, as a neighbor and friend for several years, and his poem on "The Emperor Constantine" fits here.

I could have lived in the time of Constantine.
Three hundred years after the death of the Savior,
Of whom no more was known than that he had risen
Like a sunny Mithra among Roman legionnaires.
I would have witnessed the quarrel between homoousios *and*
    homoiousios
About whether the Christ nature is divine or only resembles
    divinity.
Probably I would have cast my vote against Trinitarians,
For who could ever guess the Creator's nature?
Constantine, Emperor of the World, coxcomb and murderer,
Tipped the scale at the Council of Nicea,
So that we, generation after generation, meditate on the Holy
    Trinity,
Mystery of mysteries, without which
The blood of man would have been alien to the blood of the
    universe
And the spilling of His own blood by a suffering God, who
    offered Himself
As a sacrifice even as He was creating the world, would have
    been in vain.

Thus Constantine was merely an undeserving tool,
Unaware of what he was doing for people of distant times.

And us, do we know what we are destined for?

Life Everlasting

Life everlasting is another doctrine central to Christianity—a doctrine that many people today struggle with. Modernity, as we have seen, arrived with the discovery of empirical science, which assumes that matter (which is all science can get its hands on) is the fundamental reality in the universe, and that consciousness—more broadly speaking, sentience, but we will stay with the conventional word—is an epiphenomenon, wholly dependent on matter. This is a mistake: as we saw earlier, science misread absence-of-evidence regarding what lay outside its range as evidence-of-absence—that is, as evidence that what it can't deal with doesn't exist. The truth is that consciousness is the foundation of things. And just as matter cannot be destroyed—it can oscillate between corporeality and energy, but it cannot be annihilated—so too with consciousness. The pictures on the television screen change, but the light of the screen is constantly present to illumine them. So life is everlasting.

This may not come as good news to everybody. Those who have not had happy lives might rightfully wonder what solace there is in prolonging an unhappy experience forever. But this does not alter the fact that the "light on the television screen" never goes out. The concept of unhappy experiences being prolonged forever raises the question of damnation and hell, to which we will return shortly.

The Resurrection of the Body

The doctrine of the resurrection of the body is a bit more complex than life everlasting, but not much. It was pointed out earlier that Jesus's resurrected body was not his corpse resuscitated nor is the resurrected body that the Apostles' Creed affirms. St. Paul stated this clearly when he pointed out that "flesh and blood cannot inherit the kingdom of God," and Jesus anticipated him. When the Sadducees, who did not believe in resurrection, tried to trick him by saying that if resurrection were true, remarried widows would find themselves with multiple husbands in heaven, Jesus informed them that in heaven there is neither marriage nor betrothal, for the resurrected are, like angels, without gender.

What the doctrine of the resurrection of the body affirms is that what survives death is not a disembodied soul that is withdrawn from the body like a piston from its syringe. It resembles Aristotle's *anima* (soul), which is the agent that activates and organizes a body, whether that body is vegetable, animal, or rational, and adds to these the *resurrected* body for the anima/soul to work with. Eternal life is not simply a prolongation of *this* life, which as we have seen many would not regard as an attractive prospect. It is life of a higher order than life on earth; a life that can be obtained only through death and resurrection and that, though we can and must begin to enter upon it now, can be consummated only in eternity.

Hell

Is the resurrected body in paradise? Not necessarily. Satan may have seduced a soul into its camp, in which case that soul's resurrected body will find itself in hell, a place that is perhaps a greater mystery to us than heaven. The following questions are commonly asked:

- *What might hell be like?* Hell is popularly depicted as a fiery furnace whose flames do not consume bodies but torture them forever. But this is only a metaphor; it cannot be literally true, for resurrected bodies are incorporeal and do not have flesh that could be burned. (Remember that resurrection is not resuscitation.) The theological definition of hell is total aloneness—not being connected to anything.

I once taught a seminar on St. Augustine, and when we came to his account of this condition, one of the students found it so terrifying that she had a mental breakdown and had to drop out of school for the rest of the semester. I went to visit her, and she spoke in images of science fiction. Her fear was that if she were damned, she would be banished for eternity on some distant planet with no means of communicating with anything or anyone. She was experiencing existentially the theological meaning of hell.

- *Who is responsible for someone's being in hell?* The answer is, the individual in question. The reason for a person's being in hell is that he so consistently put himself ahead of others in his life that his capacity for empathy, his bridge to others, broke down. And he himself has caused its breakdown. Being only second in command, Satan has the power to seduce but not to compel. He cannot take away our God-given freedom.

- *Will anyone remain in hell forever?* The answer is no, for nothing can deprive us of the *imago Dei* that is the foundation of our humanity. It will keep sending us signals. We can let our willfulness suppress them or brush them aside, but for only so long. And when they begin to get through to us, our recovery is on its way. They will build on one another and increase in strength.

The Virgin Birth

The final tenet we come to in this itemization of Christian doctrines is the virgin birth. In a surprising way, it brings Christian theology full circle. The virgin birth begins Christian theology and the resurrection of the body closes it, but they are both concerned with the body.

As I keep repeating, we cannot know what actually happens on the transcendental plane; we can only try to get a handle, via formulas, on what happens. The virgin birth is one such formula. It doesn't tell us literally what happened on the physical, anatomical plane, but its metaphorical meaning, purity, is easy to see. The vessel does not contaminate what is poured into it. So the doctrine of the virgin birth proclaims that God entered mortal life uncontaminated. St. Velimirovich extended the doctrine to everyone:

O my soul, my eternal surprise, what happened once in heaven [God's existence] and once on earth [Christ's appearance] must happen to you. You must become a virgin so that the Spirit of God may fall in love with you. All the miracles in heaven and on earth originate from the Virgin and the Spirit.

APOCALYPSE: THE REVELATION TO JOHN

At first glance the virgin birth seems like an odd way to move toward the close of the Christian story, but on second thought it makes perfect sense. God launched the Christian story by entering Mary's womb, so in returning to that entry this book brings its telling of the Christian story full circle.

The last book of the Bible is commonly called Revelation, but its actual title is The Revelation to John. Christ sent an angel to reveal to John what was soon to happen, and John sent what was revealed to him in letters to the seven churches in Asia with this preface:

Look! He is coming with the clouds:
Every eye will see him.
I am the Alpha and the Omega, says the Lord God,
who is and who was and who is to come,
the Almighty.

John then tells the churches the circumstances of the revelation he is about to report. "I was on the island called Patmos," he says, "and I was in a trance, caught up in the Spirit on the Lord's day. And I heard behind me a loud voice like a trumpet saying, 'Write what you see and send it to the seven churches.'" That said, John proceeds to tell each church what he was shown and told to report to it.

Common themes run through all of the messages: God is aware of the churches' patience and perseverance, but also of their lapses—that they have let their mutual love decline, and so forth. But the heart of the letters are the reports of what John was *shown*. The revelations made to him after the trumpetlike voice told him, "Come up here, and I will show you what will take place," are brilliantly visual. When John tells us what he was shown (describing his vision in the present tense), we find ourselves back with the throne mysticism of Paul's conversion experience. For

there in heaven stood a throne, with one seated on the throne! And he who sat there appeared like jasper and carnelian, and round the throne there was a rainbow that looked like emerald. Round the throne were twenty-four thrones, and seated on the thrones were twenty-four elders, clad in white robes, with golden crowns on their heads. From the throne issued flashes of lightning, and voices and peals of thunder, and before the throne burned seven torches of fire, which were the seven spirits of God; and in front of the throne there was as it were a sea of glass, like crystal.

The descriptions go on and on, but the storyline of Revelation is impending disasters followed by final salvation. The disasters are described graphically. They are prefaced by the famed Four Horsemen of the Apocalypse ("apocalypse" being a synonym for "revelation"), who spread disaster across the earth. Their doings will be followed by scourges as numerous as locusts and more horrible than the dragons that will sweep over the earth; to these tortures will be added scorpion stings and killings with sulphurous fumes and fire. All this is orchestrated by "the beast" who is Satan's deputy on earth and whose ultimate object is to kill the child who is destined to rule the earth.

The object of these alarming descriptions is God's attempt to knock some sense into the peoples of the world and bring them to repent of their ways and reverse their stampede toward doom. The hope is not fulfilled, so God closes history down. His historical experiment is a failure, we might say— but when we step back a pace and see the larger canvas, we see that it is not. The last book of the New Testament closes with a triumphal vision:

Then I saw a new heaven and a new earth; for the first heaven and the first earth had passed away.... And I saw the holy city, new Jerusalem, coming out of heaven from God.... And I heard a great voice from the throne saying, "Behold, the dwelling of God is with men. He will dwell with them and they shall be his people, and God himself will be with them; he will wipe away every tear from their eyes, and death shall be no more, neither shall there be mourning or crying nor pain any more, for the former things have passed away.

Thus ends the primary text of the Christian story. This book's attempt to tell that story in contemporary idiom has been driven throughout by the biblical original. Now, having quoted the way the original narrative ends, I must bring the section in hand to a close.

CONCLUSION

The Christian story is the story of how "God became man so man might become God" (Irenaeus). This "becoming God" happens individually, communally, and cosmically. The first two divinizations are directions rather than destinations— sanctity in the case of individuals, and in the case of the church the degree to which, congregation by congregation, it brings the Mystical Body of Christ to life in its midst.

Cosmically, though, the divinization is categorical and assured from the start, for we belong to God and nothing can overpower the Almighty to which we belong. If we try to mastermind specifics we are out of our depth from the start, but the consensus of centuries of theological ponderings seems to be that it will occur at the end of history when time closes down and God draws his creation back into himself. He will not withdraw it into his singularity. Rather, its manifold nature will be retained with its dross transmuted into gold.

There remains the question of whether this final redemption of history is prefigured within history, and the answer is yes. An analogy and a recollection are helpful here.

The analogy is the sky. Whether it is decked out in cloud-scapes, strewn with stars, or tinted a pure empyrean blue, the sky is invariably peaceful and beautiful; it can be hid by leaden rain clouds, but these do not affect the sky itself. And it is always with us. Even when it is obscured, we know that it is there.

The temporal counterpart of the sky is eternity. It too is peaceful and beautiful, whereas history is anything but. And just as the sky enfolds the earth, eternity enfolds history. Both eternity and sky can take the initiative in calling themselves to our attention. Even when our minds are on other things, the sky can suffuse our experiences with sunlight or rain, and likewise eternity can break into the moments of our experience with lightning flashes of illumination.

It does this most noticeably by saying no to history's moments. We are so caught up in history that we forget that, taken as freestanding, history is unredeemable. To say that hope and history are always light-years apart is an understatement—they are incommensurate, for between finitude and the Infinite there is no common measure. Periodically, eternity breaks into history to remind us that history cannot stand on its own feet. First eternity pronounces its "no" on freestanding history, and then it draws history to its bosom and enfolds it with its "yes"—smothers it in its peace and beauty.

Eternity can also break into our moments of daily preoccupation like flashes of lightning on a dark night. ("Something broke and something opened. / I filled up like a new wineskin," said writer Anne Dillard.) A friend of ours who is a therapist told us recently of how she had witnessed such an opening in her office the day before:

A client had come for her weekly appointment more than usually depressed. It had been the week of her birthday and she had not heard from any of the family she had grown up in. They had become fundamentalists and thought she was damned. "My mother died last year and now I've lost the rest of them. It makes me sick," she said, too tight with pain to cry.

Then, after an unusually long silence, she murmured quietly as if to herself, "Something is happening to me." Her hands, which had been clenched in angry fists, now lay open on her lap and tears were streaming down her cheeks. Then, "I'm feeling something wonderful. Something wonderful has entered this room. It just came, didn't it?" She found herself laughing, though she tried to suppress it because it seemed inappropriate.

"I'm going to take the initiative and write to *them*," she said. "Shoot affectionate greetings to them like paper airplanes."

Sometimes intimations of eternity seem simply to drop from heaven into our laps, as Czeslaw Milosz registers in his poem "Gift":

A day so happy.
Fog lifted early. I worked in the garden.
Hummingbirds were stopping over the honeysuckle flowers.
There was no thing on earth I wanted to possess.
I knew no one worth my envying him.
Whatever evil I had suffered, I forgot.
To think that once I was the same man did not embarrass me.
In my body I felt no pain.
When straightening up, I saw blue sea and sails.

And from an anonymous poet:

I am so filled with ghosts of loveliness
That I could furbish out and populate a distant star,
So the gods could congregate to gaze, and
memorize, and duplicate.

And now we turn from personal experiences back to eternity's breakthroughs into history. These come to our attention first (as was said) in the judgment they pronounce on history's plans and projects, for the staple of history is misfortune.

Several months before the moment that I write these words I had an unusual experience, one that I had never had before. I was flying from California to Kansas City, and night had fallen when the pilot announced over the intercom that if we looked out our windows we would see a once-in-a-lifetime sight. We were flying four thousand feet above normal cruising altitude to avoid a violent thunderstorm that was sweeping across western Kansas, he explained. I looked out my window and was indeed astonished. I was looking down on an unbroken sea of light, but light of a kind I had never before seen—Wordsworth's "light that never was on sea or land." It was so ethereal that simply to gaze on it was to feel peaceful. It is no exaggeration to say that it was a holy light.

This is the way eternity redeems time's moment-by-moment flow. The light I was gazing on was consummately peaceful and beautiful, as is eternity. But if it were to disclose its fullness, history would vanish in an instant. We are back with Emily Dickinson's "Like lightning to the children eased /

Through revelation kind, / The truth must dazzle gradually / Or every man be blind." So the sea of holy light held itself in check and fell on the flatlands of Kansas in brilliant zig-zag streaks that were not only spectacular but could be smelled as they enriched the earth's atmosphere and water by adding nitrogen to it.

When, on one occasion, our six-year-old grandson stepped outdoors after a thunderstorm, he exclaimed, "I like this air!"

That would be an appropriate ending to this part of the book, but I will ask St. Paul to pronounce the benediction for it:

> I bow my knees unto the Father . . . that according to the riches of his glory he may grant you to be strengthened with might through his Spirit in the inner man, and that Christ may dwell in your hearts by faith; that you, being rooted and grounded in love, may have power to comprehend with all the saints what is the breadth, and length and height and depth, and to know the love of Christ, which surpassed knowledge, that you may be filled with the fullness of God.

Part Three

THE THREE MAIN BRANCHES OF CHRISTIANITY TODAY

The body of this book addresses Christianity as a whole. This does not mean that every Christian will agree with all that has been said; Christianity is such a complex phenomenon that it is difficult to say anything significant about it that will carry the assent of all Christians. So it must be stressed that what has gone before is an interpretation. Nevertheless, it has sought to be an interpretation of the points that, substantially at least, Christians hold in common.

When we turn from the Christianity of the first millennium, its Great Tradition, to Christendom today, we find the church divided into three great branches. Roman Catholicism focuses on the Vatican in Rome and spreads out from there, being dominant in Poland, central and southern Europe, Ireland, and South America. Eastern Orthodoxy has its major influence in Greece, the Slavic countries, and Russia. Protestantism dominates northern Europe, England, Scotland, and North America.

Up to the year 313 the Christian church struggled in the face of official Roman persecution. In that year it became legally recognized and enjoyed equal rights with other religions of the empire. Before the century was out, in 380, Christianity became the official religion of the Roman Empire. With a few minor splinterings, such as the Nestorians (who believed that Christ was of a similar substance as God but not the same substance) and the Mar Toma Church in India (still a viable institution, which believes that it was founded by Jesus's disciple Thomas), it continued as a united body up to 1054. This means that for roughly half its history the church remained substantially one institution.

In 1054, however, its first great division occurred in the Christian church, between groups that would become the Eastern Orthodox Church in the East and the Roman Catholic Church in the West. The reasons for the break were complex—geography, culture, language, and politics as well as religion were involved. The next great division occurred in the Catholic Church with the Protestant Reformation in the sixteenth century. Protestantism followed four main courses—Baptist, Lutheran, Calvinists, and Anglican—which themselves subdivided until the current census lists over nine hundred denominations in the United States alone. Currently, the ecumenical movement is bringing some of these denominations back together again.

With these minimum facts at our disposal, we can proceed to our real concern, which is to try to understand the central perspectives of Christendom's three great branches, beginning with the Roman Catholic Church.

ROMAN CATHOLICISM

We shall confine ourselves here to what are perhaps the two most important concepts for the understanding of this branch of Christendom: the Church as teaching authority, and the Church as sacramental agent.

Authority

The Catholic vision is radically personal: the Church is the communion of humans who are being initiated into the life of the Blessed Trinity, the three persons who are one God, and who are archetypes of personhood—complete persons—that human beings approximate but whose fullness they fall short of. And this vision is also radically incarnational: God becomes man through a human being, through a human mother, a woman who has been held in special veneration by the Catholic faithful from earliest times. This communion of God and man, with its preparation through the history of humanity and of Israel in particular, reaches its apex in Mary, who is the perfect "receiver of the Word" (that is, Jesus). Mary is seen in the Catholic view as incorporating in her self the history of her people, through which God was planning to redeem the world. Mary was prepared for her mission by the mysterious workings of grace, and she freely assented to God's plan by her assent to become the mother of God. God was recreating the fallen world—and this through the human agency of Mary.

God, of course, is the ultimate "authority," for only God is the "author," the source and origin of all that is. He has, as it were, "author's rights" over the story being told in and through creation and the ages that have followed. Part of his loving plan, part of his total generosity, is setting human freedom at the center of the work of redemption. And that freedom blossoms in the "yes" of Mary to God's invitation that she become the mother of his Son. Because of this, she is the first and greatest disciple, with an authority transcending all other authority in the Church. It is an authority prior to that of office, a silent authority rooted in an obedience to God that underlies all authority. Mary is at the contemplative heart of the Catholic Church, where heaven and earth meet in Jesus.

Tradition sees the Church formed at the foot of the Cross where Mary is given as mother to the "beloved disciple," who in turn is given to her as son. The relations are familial—a new family, the family of faith, the family into which will be inducted all those who have left everything for the sake of Jesus. In this "new family" the following of Christ in poverty, chastity, and obedience in a life of consecrated virginity is seen as the "counsel of perfection" for those who would follow Christ most fully. In Mary, and in her alone, this virginal consecration was combined with the tremendous dignity of human motherhood.

It was the Holy Spirit who came upon Mary when she conceived the Son of God. At the end of his life, after Jesus returned to the Father in the Ascension, the Holy Spirit descended again upon Mary. But this time, Pentecost, she was surrounded by different groups of followers of Jesus—the apostles, his blood relatives, the women. Through these groups we see various "constellations of holiness" in which the Holy Spirit continues and expands the incarnation of Jesus in the world.

Even as he, the seed of God, fell into the earth and died, so he bears rich fruit through the ages. The Catholic sees the Church as the Bride of Christ, and sees its type in the Virgin Mary, who has been venerated through the millennia as "Virgin, Mother, and Bride." Throughout the Bible, God has insisted on fruitfulness: "Be fruitful and multiply; by this my Father is glorified; that you bear much fruit and so prove to be my disciples." This fruit culminates in the lives of the saints— human beings who already in this life become transparent to the light of God as it breaks into this present age, the world today. Saints fully realize the missions given them by God, missions which make them theological persons in their own right, even as the Son is on a mission from the Father, even as he finds sustenance in doing the will of the Father. The saints are the glory of the Church, for in them alone the baptismal promises are fully realized. They are "the Church triumphant." In them alone is the Church fully herself. On earth, the Church pursues its pilgrim's way, for which the saying "Many are called but few are chosen" remains a constant admonition.

Though mystical gifts abound in the life of the Church, they are given to build up the faith of the Body of Christ. It is obedience to the will of the Father that is the "food of Jesus," and it is obedience which is to be the characteristic of his Body, his Bride, which is the Church. As we have seen, there is a unique authority that flows from the person of the Mother of God, she who was the "perfect yes" to God's call and whose Son is also "all yes" to God.

The Church is a family—a new family—and there is authority within the family. There is an authority of office vested in Peter, who was publicly selected by Jesus to be chief shepherd of the flock and "prince of the apostles." Peter's statement of faith—a grace filled, supernatural recognition of who Jesus was—revealed that God was at work in him, and Jesus in turn recognized him as "the rock" on whom he would build his Church. To Peter was given the "power of the keys." Peter was hardly a superman. John was clearly closer to the Lord, and the great mystic among the disciples. Paul was a better missionary, theologian. and mystic. Peter denied knowing the Lord, and the Gospels show him as impetuous to the point of folly. Yet the one who was raised in a carpenter's workshop and chose the fishermen gave Peter the dignity that led to his being the first Bishop of Rome, the first Pope.

"Papa" is a loving appellation given to fathers; and in the case of the "Papa" of Rome this title has stuck: the mantle which fell upon Peter has been passed on to his successors for two millennia. To be the "Vicar of Christ" and "Servant of the Servants of God" has not always been easy. The Papacy has taken on many characteristics through the centuries, various styles of leadership in many ways reflecting the styles of princely leadership of the time. The office itself is seen as having the final responsibility for preserving the "deposit of faith"—for seeing to it that the "mystery hidden for ages and generations but now manifest to his saints" be kept whole and pure throughout time. The office is always bigger than the man, and sometimes vastly so. Some popes have been scandalous sinners; many have been saints. Peter was both in his time.

From the days of the first councils, when parts of the "deposit of faith" have come under attack or have been exaggerated, the teaching office of the Church—the "magisterium"—has sought to articulate and define truths which until the particular crisis had been taken for granted. Though infallibility had been acknowledged in word and practice from the time of Clement of Rome (see his Letter to the Corinthians, A.D. 95), in the mid-nineteenth century the Church officially defined the circumstances under which it speaks infallibly. When on issues of faith and morality the Church senses that confusion is rearing its head, it offsets the confusion by saying categorically where the truth lies. Thereafter any such pronouncements are a canonized part of Catholic doctrine and are no longer open to dispute. Underlining the responsibility of the successor of Peter to keep the Gospel whole and pure, the Church also carefully distinguished between the "ordinary teaching office" of the Pope and the "extraordinary office," in which as the successor of Peter he speaks infallibly.

Representing a kingship "not of this world," the Papal Church has been a thorn in the side of the powers of this world—empires and kingdoms right up to modern tyrannies like those of Nazis and Communists who slated the Church for destruction. The Church has emerged from the ruins of atheistic modernity crowned with saints. The twentieth century has been her greatest age of martyrs.

Mindful of "Christ poor and humiliated," the Church has always had a "preferential option" for the poor, witnessed to by scores of saints. In modern times this devotion to the poor has grown into a veritable treasure house of social teachings and a profound commitment to social justice. This commitment has been lived in many ways, from the sacrificial work of Mother Teresa of Calcutta, to the giving of his life for another by Auschwitz martyr St. Maximilian Kolbe, to Dorothy Day's unflagging devotion to the homeless on the streets of New York City.

In the twentieth century the Church has emerged as a defender of all human life. The Catholic Church has always insisted on the goodness of creation, yet with no illusions. Droughts, earthquakes, and floods can cause enormous damage, but the Church stands by its conviction in the goodness of nature. This results from the insistence on the redemption of humanity—and the world—effected by the Incarnation, and leads to the tension of being "in the world but not of it." Likely the most common symbol in Catholicism is the crucifix: the center of meditation being the fully human body of Jesus Christ, crucified by the world, the fullest expression of God's boundless love for the world. Only a profound trust in the Resurrection can allow this steady and unblinking contemplation of what the world is really about as revealed in the ignominy of the Cross, a trust which will not rest until "the darkness of Calvary yields to final victory."

The authority which Christ explicitly gave his Church, he gave to the apostles in Peter. Together, they set out to spread the good news throughout the world. That good news was spread by the authority of the "author" himself, Jesus, who was with them, confirming "the message by the signs that attend it." Though the public revelation was sealed with the death of Jesus's last disciple, infallibility, Catholics believe, is something that is guaranteed to the entire Church. And it is the task of that Church to teach and preach its good news to every age, to witness to the entire world Christ's life, death and resurrection. It is the authority of the apostolic Church that formed the Christian Bible, and it is the authority of the apostles that enables believers to trust that biblical teaching. The "author" has given power to support the Church in these ways to his apostles, gathered around Peter. And yet Peter has a responsibility that is uniquely his: individual apostles can fall away, and have fallen away, but the rock that is Peter has held.

Though divine in origin, the Church is made up of humans, of sinners, and so in an act unique for any institution, at the end of the second millennium the Pope publicly apologized and did penance in the name of the Church for the sins of individual Christians throughout the ages.

Throughout the ages, the Vatican City in Rome has stood as a symbol of unity and continuity with the apostles Peter and Paul. However, the authority of the "petrine" office of the Pope is not tied to the actual buildings of the Vatican City. The living center of the Church is found in every tabernacle of the world where, in the sacrament of the Eucharist, Christians encounter Christ's "Real Presence." This leads us directly to a discussion of the sacraments.

The Sacraments

The fountain of the sacramental life of the Church is the pierced side of Jesus, from which flow the twin streams of blood and water, symbols of the washing waters of *baptism* and of the *Eucharist*. The other sacraments cluster around these two moments. In baptism, as in *confession* and later in *anointing the body as it approaches death,* it is the "forgiveness of sins" which is effected in the life of the believer: it is in this the Church extends Jesus's mission of forgiving sins through the ages. In the Eucharist, communion is established between God and man. This "communion" is at the very heart of the Church.

To receive the Eucharist and thereby be in "communion" with God, one must have the proper disposition, for the Eucharist is an "open secret" to those whose eyes have been purified by the sacramental forgiveness of sins, and who, receiving in the obedience of faith, can taste the delights of heaven come to earth. The Eucharist is a "standing miracle" effected at every Mass celebrated in the world, for in it, Catholics believe, the bread and wine are actually transformed into the very "body, blood, soul, and divinity" of Jesus Christ. The future life—everlasting life—is present in this heart of all sacramental life. This belief is so essential that some of the Eucharistic bread is kept in a special repository, a "tabernacle," in every Catholic place of prayer where it is adored. It is the Real Presence of Christ, the living link between heaven and earth.

The miracle of the Eucharist takes place at the liturgy commonly called the Mass, celebrated by a successor of the apostles or his ordained representative.* It is for this reason that Catholics treasure the gift of the priesthood. Even though the entire Catholic Church is a "nation of priests," a "priestly

---

* The word "Mass" derives from the same root, the Latin *missa*, as the English word "dismiss." The closing words of the Mass, *Ite, missa est,* mean (in intent), "Go, the Church has been sent." To which the congregation responds, *Deo gratias,* "Thanks be to God."

people," there are men chosen from the community to live the hierarchical priesthood for the community, to embody/model Christ in a special way for God's people. They are elevated to this by the sacrament of *Holy Orders*. Though there have been married priests throughout history, the desire for the closest possible imitation of Christ in unmarried chastity has formed a strong preference for the celibate priesthood. The fullness of the sacrament is found in the bishop, of whom the priest is really a representative collaborator.

The parting of ways with the traditional religion of Israel is seen in controversies over the Jerusalem Temple. Jesus worshipped in the Temple, as did his immediate followers. Still, there were controversies as to what was the *true* Temple, and Jesus predicted that a day would come when the Temple in Jerusalem would no longer be the center of the cult of God. That day came in A.D. 70, when the Temple was destroyed. Christians had come to see in Jesus the true Temple, "not made by human hands," and they came to see his sacrificial death on Calvary as bringing to perfection all the sacrifices of ancient Israel. So Christians see a new Temple in the body of Jesus, and it is his body that is the inclusive sacrifice, reenacted throughout the ages in every Mass in the world.

When a child comes to the age of understanding, the sacrament of *confirmation* secures the blessing of baptism by anchoring it in comprehending minds. Recalling the Holy Spirit sent upon the early Church at Pentecost, the anointing of confirmation introduces a youth into the ongoing priesthood of the faithful.

Though mindful of the consequences of the fall, the Catholic faith has a positive view of the created world: theologically stated, "grace builds on nature without destroying it." Thus it is characteristically Catholic to recognize and celebrate *marriage* as a sacrament. In it, that which is the pinnacle of human love is touched by, blessed, and elevated by the love of God. The sacrament of marriage offers the promise that human desire can phase into the love of God. The Hebrew Bible sees God as the "Bridegroom of Israel," and Christians see that Bridegroom as having come to earth. Catholics see the relation of Christ to His Church as the model for marriage. Jesus's first miracle took place at a wedding feast, and indirectly he blesses all marriages through that ceremony. Thus this most natural and human of institutions shares in the very life of Heaven and reveals something of the perfect and fruitful love of Heaven to earth.

The Church, then, sees herself as the Mystical Body of Christ, a body that was first formed of the flesh and blood of one woman, Mary, who flawlessly lived the obedience of faith and who was raised to a peak of holiness far above angels and saints. Yet Mary remains human—the perfection of humanity—even as she brings to humanity God-made-man in her son. Through these human persons God creates a new humanity, and because "the dwelling place of God is with men," it is in this humanity that he is creating a "new heaven and a new earth." The Church is the "People of God" moving through history.

With the Second Vatican Council in the 1960s, the Catholic Church sought to remove impediments to dialogue with modern people of goodwill, opening herself to richer relations with both other Christian communities and with the world. Twenty years after that Council, for the first time in millennia, a Pope was selected from a land that had never been part of the Roman Empire. Dominantly though not exclusively Latin for fifteen hundred years, the Church is dramatically returning to a representatively global presence, seeking to define a new role for Peter as servant of unity among all Christians and people of goodwill.

To expand somewhat on the positive understanding of the relations of the Catholic Church with other communions that has followed the Vatican Council, the metaphor of "communion" has emerged as central for expressing the Christian mystery. To be in "full communion" or in "partial communion" expresses the degrees of a Christian's relation to the Catholic Church. The "Catholica"—those who are in full communion—do not hold a majority position, for it is restricted to the total wholeness of saints. In practice the Catholic Church is now seeing herself more as a communion of local Churches who are in full communion with the successor of Peter.

The Catholic Church has always recognized the power of God at work outside her visible confines: the early Fathers spoke of the *logoi spermatikoi,* the "seed words" scattered throughout creation. The Church seeks to celebrate and indeed foster whatever is good and true in any religious tradition and culture, hoping to lead all to an appreciation of the fullness of truth revealed in Jesus Christ and in His Bride, the Church.

By the beginning of the third millennium, many traditionally Catholic lands in western Europe had long ceased to be strongly Christian, even as this had happened in the first millennium in North Africa and much of the Near East. Emerging from the devastation of the twentieth century—the new age of martyrs—a vibrant and numerically strong Catholicism is emerging in parts of central and eastern Europe, in parts of Africa, and in the Philippines, Korea, and Vietnam. Catholicism is the largest Christian body in both North and South America and Oceania; and in western Europe, though greatly vitiated by secularism, Catholicism has a significant presence.

EASTERN ORTHODOXY

The Eastern Orthodox Church, which today has somewhere in the neighborhood of 250 million communicants, broke officially with the Roman Catholic Church in 1054, each charging the other with responsibility for the break. Eastern Orthodoxy includes the churches of Albania, Bulgaria, Georgia, Greece, Romania, Russia, Serbia, and Sinai. While each of these churches is self-governing, they are to varying degrees in communion with one another, and their members think of themselves as belonging primarily to the Eastern Church and only secondarily to their particular divisions within it.

In most ways the Eastern Orthodox Church stands close to the Roman Catholic, for during almost half their histories they constituted a single body. It honors the sacraments, though it has never specified their number, and interprets them in fundamental respects exactly as does the Roman Church. On the teaching authority there is some difference, but even here the premise is the same. Left to private interpretation the Christian faith would disintegrate into conflicting claims and a chaos of uncertainties. It is the church's responsibility to ensure against this, and God enables it to do so; the Holy Spirit preserves its official statements against error. This much is shared with Rome.

The differences between Orthodoxy and Catholicism on the subject of authority are two. The first of these has to do with extent. The Eastern Church considers the issues on which unanimity is needed to be fewer than does the Roman Church. In principle, only issues that are mentioned in scripture can qualify—which is to say, the church can *interpret* doctrines but it cannot *initiate* them. In practice the Eastern Church has exercised her prerogative as interpreter only seven times, in the seven Ecumenical Councils, all of which were held before 787. This means that the Eastern Church assumes that though the articles of faith that Christians must believe are decisive, their number is relatively few. Specifically, it does not subscribe to the immaculate conception (the view that Mary was conceived in her mother's womb without original sin) and denies that there is a purgatory (which the Roman Church conceives as a temporary abode where souls are punished for sins that have not yet been forgiven). Catholics regard these dogmas and others, like the bodily assumption of Mary, positively, as the development of doctrine, whereas Orthodox Christians consider them innovations. (In passing, Catholics visually depict the full body of Christ, whereas Orthodox Christians consider this as bordering on idolatry and show him in paintings and, at most, bas relief.)

Generalizing on the differences, we can say that the Latin Church stresses the development of Christian doctrine, whereas the Greek Church stresses its continuity. What is referred to as "the magisterium of the academy" enters into this difference, for nothing like the great university centers of Bologna and Paris characterizes the Eastern experience. (The closest equivalent might be Byzantium at its height, with its magnificent cathedrals and fabled art collections that continue to tour the great museums of the world.) We think of the Middle Ages as the golden age of Roman Catholicism, whereas for Eastern Christianity we reach back to the church fathers.

The other way in which the Eastern Church's understanding of its role as teaching authority differs from Catholicism lies in the means by which its dogmas are reached. The Roman Church, as we have seen, holds that in the final analysis dogmas come through the pope; it is in the decisions that he announces that the Holy Spirit preserves from error. The Eastern Church has no pope and holds that God's truth is disclosed through "the conscience of the church," using this phrase to refer to the consensus of Christians generally. This consensus needs, of course, to be focused, which is what ecclesiastical councils were for. When the bishops of the entire early church assembled in the seven Ecumenical Councils, their collective judgment established God's truth in their unchangeable monuments. It would be correct to say that the Holy Spirit preserved their decisions from error, but it would be truer to the spirit of the Eastern Church to say that the Holy Spirit preserved Christian minds as a whole from lapsing into error, for bishops' decisions are assumed to do no more than focus the decisions of all Christians.

This brings us to one of the special emphases of the Eastern Church. Because in many ways it stands midway between Roman Catholicism and Protestantism, it is more difficult to put one's finger on features within it that are clearly distinctive; but if we were to select two (as we did in our sketch of

Roman Catholicism), one of these would be its exceptionally corporate view of the church. The other, which we will come to shortly, is its emphasis on mysticism.

The Corporate View of the Church

Common to all Christians is the view of the church as the Mystical Body of Christ. Just as the parts of the body are joined in common well-being or malaise, so too are the lives of Christians interrelated. All Christians accept the doctrine that they are "members of one another." But while matters of degree are notoriously difficult to determine, it could be argued that the Eastern Church has taken this notion more seriously than either Roman Catholicism or Protestantism. Each Christian is working out his or her salvation in conjunction with the rest of the church, not individually to save a separate soul. "One can be damned alone, but saved only with others" is a familiar adage in the Russian Church.

The Holy Spirit enters every individual soul as a cell in the Mystical Body of Christ. But individual cells cannot survive without other cells to work with. And Orthodoxy takes seriously St. Paul's theme of the entire universe "groaning in travail" as it awaits redemption. Orthodoxy brings the entire universe into the economy of salvation. Not only is the destiny of the individual bound up with the entire church; the church is responsible for helping to sanctify the entire world of nature and history. The welfare of everything in creation is affected to some degree by what each individual soul contributes to or detracts from it.

Mystical Emphasis

The experiential consequence of this strong corporeal feeling is that mysticism figures more prominently in the East than in the West. This comes to light when we ask to what extent it should be a part of the Christian program to try to partake of supernatural life while here on earth.

The Roman Church holds that the Trinity dwells in every Christian soul, but its presence is not normally felt. By a life of prayer and penance it is possible to dispose oneself for a special gift by which the Trinity discloses its presence and the seeker is lifted to a state of mystical ecstasy. But because as human beings we have no right to such states (the states being wholly in the nature of free gifts of grace) the Roman Church neither urges nor discourages their cultivation.

The Eastern Church, on the other hand, actively encourages the mystical life. From very early times, when the deserts near Antioch and Alexandria were filled with hermits seeking illumination, the mystical enterprise has occupied a more prominent place in its life. Because the supernatural world intersects and impregnates the world of sense throughout, it should be a part of Christian life in general to develop the capacity to experience directly the glories of God's presence; in the Christian East, the concept of "one who is able to speak about God on the basis of direct experience" is built into the very definition of "theologian," and St. John the Evangelist, author of the most mystical and theological of the Gospels, is judged to be among the top three in this category, St. Gregory of Nazianzus and Symeon the New Theologian being the other two.

The British poet Francis Thompson was not Orthodox, but some lines by him put their finger on the Eastern Church's mystical emphasis so well that they merit quoting here:

Does the fish soar to find the ocean,
The eagle plunge to find the air,
That we ask of the stars in motion
If they have rumour of thee there?

Not where the wheeling systems darken,
And our benumbed conceiving soars,
The drift of pinions, would we harken,
Beats at our own clay-shuttered doors.

The angels keep their ancient places;
Turn but a stone, and start a wing:
'Tis ye, 'tis your estranged faces
That miss the many-splendoured thing.

The desert hermits gave their whole lives to lessening the estrangement of their faces, and the aim of every life, says the Orthodox Church, should be union with God—actual deification, becoming through grace "partakers of the divine nature." *Theosis* is the Greek word for this partaking, and every Christian should try to make life a pilgrimage toward its glory.

There is a nineteenth-century classic of Russian spirituality, *The Way of a Pilgrim,* that describes one seeker's search for this grace with such unassuming modesty and winsomeness that it has made its way into the hearts of Christians everywhere and belongs to the world.

When the pilgrim comes to us in the pages of his lovely book, we don't know who he is any more than we do when he leaves us a short one hundred pages later. He doesn't tell us his name. We learn only that he is thirty-three years old, has a withered arm, and walks unendingly carrying a knapsack that holds only dry bread, his Bible, and the *Philokalia* (literally, "The Love of Beauty"), a collection of writings by the church fathers which shows the way to awaken and develop attention and consciousness. The pilgrim harps on one string only— but what a string it is! It gives forth a deep-burdened sound that runs under the discords of his daily life till it brings them into harmony with God.

The pilgrim got on to this "string" through noticing, during the scripture reading in a church liturgy, three puzzling words: those in which St. Paul admonishes the Thessalonians to "pray without ceasing." How is it possible to pray without ceasing? he wondered. Still, were it not possible, the apostle would not have enjoined us to do so.

The pilgrim starts on his way. He visits many churches where famous preachers are to be heard; perhaps they can throw some light on his problem. He hears many fine sermons on prayer—what it is, how much we need it, what its fruits are—but none tells him how he can pray without ceasing.

Finally he comes on a *starets* (a man of advanced spirituality) who knows. Reaching for his copy of the *Philokalia*, the starets says, "No, it's not more sublime and holy than the Bible. But it contains clear explanations of what the Bible holds in secret. And it tells you what you are searching for, how to pray without ceasing."

The starets opens the book and reads aloud: "Sit down alone and in silence. Lower your head, shut your eyes, breathe out gently, and imagine yourself looking into your own heart. Carry your mind—that is, your thoughts—from your head to your heart. As you breathe out, say 'Lord Jesus Christ have mercy on me.'

"Say it moving your lips slowly, or simply say it in your mind," the starets adds. "Try to put all other thoughts aside. Be calm, be patient, and repeat the prayer very frequently."

The pilgrim is overjoyed with his find. The starets dismisses him with his blessing and tells him that he must return if he encounters difficulties. The pilgrim finds a garden in a nearby village and sets to work, but in three weeks he returns to the starets reporting boredom. The starets receives him, and perceiving that the pilgrim is serious he settles down to work with him in earnest. He gives him a rosary and tells him to repeat the prayer three thousand times the first day, six thousand times for the next two days, then twelve thousand times, and then without limit.

What happens this time? The first two days are difficult. After that, the prayer "becomes so easy and likable that as soon as I stopped, I felt a sort of need to go on saying it. I grew so used to my prayer that when I stopped for a single moment I felt as though something were missing, as though I had lost something. The very moment I started the prayer again, it went on easily and joyously."

The prayer begins to wake him up in the morning. It seems as if his lips and tongue pronounce the words by themselves, without any urging. He comes to feel light, as if he were walking on air. And his world is transformed:

I felt there was no happier person on earth than I, and I doubted if there could be greater and fuller happiness in the kingdom of heaven. The whole outside world also seemed to me full of charm and delight. Everything drew me to love and thank God: people, trees, plants, and animals. I saw them all as my kinfolk; I found in all of them the magic of the name of Jesus.

J. D. Salinger is best known as the author of *Catcher in the Rye,* which became a minor classic in its time for unmasking the phoniness in modern life. In its sequel, *Franny and Zooey* (which first appeared in two consecutive issues of *The New Yorker* magazine), he uses the Jesus Prayer to point the way out of that phoniness.

In Orthodoxy, a pilgrim's path leads naturally to the Holy Mountain, Mount Athos, a long, finger-thin peninsula that projects from Macedonia in northern Greece and climbs gradually for thirty-five miles until it drops precipitously into the Aegean Sea. An inaccessible mountain crest separates it from the mainland. Because of its inaccessibility and its natural beauty, it seems not to belong to this world. Thickly wooded slopes that plunge down into the deep sea, secluded coves, rocky headlands, broad bays fringed by sandy beaches, and twenty monasteries betokening bygone centuries make it one of the most beautiful landscapes in the world—the beauty of the Infinite; heaven touching earth like the tip of a rainbow.

All of the nations in Orthodoxy have their spiritual outposts in its self-governing monasteries. I will let the pilgrimage of a twentieth-century metropolitan (a dioceant bishop), Heirotheos Vlachos, carry us onto the mountain itself:

Sunset on Mount Athos—the sun was about to set, but I was ascending in order to rise. The setting of the sun found me climbing with great difficulty a narrow and steep path towards the East. I was walking bent over, the Jesus Prayer on my lips, for this is the way one should visit the Holy Mountain—having the feeling of a simple pilgrim. A short distance away from the path among the rocks one can see small houses, which are the cells of the hermit-monks. Some of them are within caves, others project a little from the face of the cliff, and you think when you look at them that they will fall into the sea. It is within these small caves that the spiritual bees live, making the sweetest honey of the hesychia—silence or stillness.

I continued my way to the heights, to the mountain of my transfiguration. After a while I reached with great effort the cell which I wanted to visit. I stood outside for a little to cool down. The cell of a hermit, I thought, is not only a place of mystery but also a heavenly place. He who dwells within and is occupied with hesychia and prayer is an Apostle of Christ.

I knocked on the outer door of the cave. Endless peace reigned, which scared me a little. Some slow steps were heard. The door opened quietly and one of the disciples who lived there appeared in front of me.

"Your blessing," I said.

"The Lord bless you," he replied.

I was moved by his presence in this wild area and by his life, his youth, in that hard place. Although I did not know him I felt admiration for him. "Are there many of you here?" I asked.

"Our spiritual elder and three disciples," he replied.

"I would like to discuss a few things that are on my mind; that is why I came here to this solitary place."

"What you have done is good," he said. "Pilgrims should come here with this sort of feeling. Some come simply out of an external curiosity, and our elder finds them very tiring."

"I would like, if it is possible, to see your elder." The disciple said he would ask, and disappeared.

In several minutes the old man appeared in front of me. It was like a sun which rose suddenly, like a spring which cascaded joy, like lightning in the night. His white beard fell like a waterfall from his face. His eyes were penetrating, shining, brilliant.

"Your blessing," I said, bending low to kiss his hand, which showed the marks of many prostrations. Yet he bent lower than I did, and was the first to give the kiss.

PROTESTANTISM

The causes that led to the break between Roman Catholicism and what came to be known as Protestant Christianity are complex and still in dispute. Political economy, nationalism, Renaissance individualism, and a rising concern over ecclesiastical abuses all played their part. They do not, however, camouflage the fact that the basic cause was religious, a difference in Christian perspective between Roman Catholicism and Protestantism. As we are concerned here with ideas rather than history, we shall say no more about the causes of the Protestant Reformation. Instead, we shall be content to treat the sixteenth century—Luther, Calvin, the Ninety-five Theses, the Diet of Worms, King Henry VIII, the Peace of Augsburg—as a vast tunnel. The Western Church entered that tunnel whole; it emerged from it in two sections. More accurately, it emerged in several sections, for Protestantism is not so much a church as a movement of churches.

The deepest differences in Protestantism today are not denominational; they are emphases that cut across denominations and often combine in the same person: fundamentalist, conservative-evangelical, mainline, charismatic, and social activist. In this brief overview we shall not go into these differences, which tend to be of recent origin. Instead, without repeating the bulk of its faith and practice, which it shares with Catholicism and Orthodoxy—Protestantism is more Christian than Protestant—we shall proceed to its two great enduring themes, with which we must here be content. They are justification by faith and the Protestant Principle.

Justification by Faith

Faith, in the Protestant conception, is not simply a matter of belief, an acceptance of knowledge held with certainty yet not on evidence. It is a response of the entire self; in Emil Brunner's phrase, "a totality-act of the whole personality." As such it does include a movement of the *mind* in assent—specifically, a conviction of God's limitless, omnipresent creative power—but this is not its all. To be truly faith it must include as well a movement of the *affections* in love and trust, and a movement of the *will* in desire to be an instrument of God's redeeming love. When Protestantism says that human beings are justified (that is, restored to right relationship with the ground of their being, and with their associates) by faith, it is saying that such restoration requires a movement of the total self, in mind, will, and affections, all three. And it must be enacted, performed. Texts are not plays and music is not music until they are performed. Just so, Christian faith is not faith until it lives, moves, and has its being in the Christian performance known as discipleship. And it is not the work of individuals. Even virtuoso soloists require performing communities to train them, sustain them, and provide orchestral backgrounds for their concerts.

At the same time, and in no way contradicting what was just said, faith is also a deeply personal matter. "Right beliefs" or "sound doctrine" can be accepted secondhand and largely by rote, but service and love cannot. Faith is the response by which God, heretofore a postulate of philosophers or theologians, becomes God for *me, my* God. This is the meaning of Luther's statement that "everyone must do his own believing as he will have to do his own dying."

To feel the force of the Protestant emphasis on faith as a response of the entire self, we need to see it as a passionate repudiation of religious perfunctoriness. Martin Luther's protest against indulgences—the medieval Catholic view that by contributing to the coffers of the church one could buy departed souls' way out of purgatory—is only a symbol of this wider protest, which extended in a number of directions. No number of religious observances, no record of good deeds, no roster of doctrines believed could guarantee that an individual would reach his or her desired state. Such things were not irrelevant to the Christian life; but unless they helped to transform the believer's heart (his or her attitudes and response to life), they were inadequate. This is the meaning of the Protestant rallying cry, "Justification by faith alone." It does not mean that the creeds or the sacraments are unimportant. It means that unless these are accompanied by the experience of God's love and a returning love for God, they are insufficient. Similarly with good works. The Protestant position does not imply that good works are unimportant. It holds that, fully understood, they are correlatives of faith rather than its preludes. If one really does have faith, good works will flow from it naturally—"Faith without works is dead" (James 2:17)—whereas the reverse cannot be assumed; that is, good works do not necessarily lead to faith. Luther lived fifteen hundred years after St. Paul, but both were driven to their emphasis on faith because a respectable string of good works, doggedly performed, had not succeeded in transforming their hearts.

Continuing with what faith is, it is participating in God's infinite love for the world. If we visualize that love as a ray of light descending from heaven, faith is moving into that light and letting it transform us to become a part of it.

We can draw here on the analogy of the child in his or her home. After the child's physical needs have been met, or rather while they are being met, the child needs above all to feel the enveloping love and acceptance of its parents. Paul, Luther, and Protestants in general say something comparable for human beings throughout their lifespans. Since from first to last human beings are vulnerable before the powers that confront them, their lifelong need is to know that their basic environment, the

THE SOUL OF CHRISTIANITY

ground of being from which they have derived and to which they will return, is *for* them rather than *against* them. If they can come to know this to the extent of really feeling it, they are released from the basic anxiety that causes them to try to elbow their way to security. This is why, just as the loved child is the cooperative child, the man or woman in whom God's love has awakened the answering response of faith is the one who can truly love other people. The key is inward. Given faith in God's goodness, everything of importance follows. In its absence, nothing can take its place.

The Protestant Principle

The other controlling perspective in Protestantism has come to be called the "Protestant Principle." Stated philosophically, it warns against absolutizing the relative. Stated theologically, it warns against idolatry.

The point is this. Human allegiance belongs to God: this all religions (with allowance for terminology) will affirm. God, however, is beyond nature and history. God is not removed from these, but the Divine cannot be equated with either of them (or any of their parts); for while the world is finite, God is infinite. With these truths all the great religions agree in principle. They are, however, very hard truths to keep in mind; so hard that people continually let them slip and proceed to equate God with something they can see or touch or at least conceptualize more precisely than the Infinite.

Early on people equated God with statues, until prophets—the first "protestants" or protesters on this score—rose up to denounce their transpositions, dubbing their pitiful substitutes idols, or "little pieces of form." Later, people stopped deifying wood and stone, but this did not mean that idolatry ended. While the secular world proceeded to absolutize the state, or the self, or human intellect, Christians fell to absolutizing dogmas, the sacraments, the church, the Bible, or personal religious experience. To think that Protestantism devalues these or doubts that God is involved in them is to misjudge it seriously. Protestantism does, however, insist that none of them is God. All, being involved in history, contain something of the human; and since the human is always imperfect, these instruments are to some degree imperfect as well. As long as they point beyond themselves to God, they can be invaluable. But let any of them claim to deserve absolute or unreserved allegiance—which is to say, claim to be God—and they become diabolical. For this, as we have seen, is what the devil is: the highest angel who, not content to be second, was determined to be first.

In the name of the sovereign God, who transcends all the limitations and distortions of finite existence, therefore, every human claim to absolute truth or finality must be rejected. Some examples will indicate what this principle means in practice. Protestants cannot accept the dogma of papal infallibility because this would involve removing from criticism forever opinions that, having been channeled through human minds, can never (in the Protestant view) wholly escape the risk of limitation and partial error. Creeds and pronouncements can be believed; indeed, they can be believed fully and wholeheartedly. But to place them beyond the cleansing crossfire of challenge and criticism is to absolutize something finite—to elevate "a little piece of form" to the position that should be reserved for God alone.

Instances of what Protestants consider idolatry are not confined to other sects or religions. Protestants admit that the tendency to absolutize the relative is universal; it occurs among them as much as it does anywhere else, bringing the need for continual self-criticism and reformation to the door of Protestantism itself. The chief Protestant idolatry has been bibliolatry. Protestants do believe that God speaks to people through the Bible as in no other way. But to elevate the Bible as a book to a point above criticism, to insist that every word and letter was dictated directly by God and so can contain no historical, scientific, or other inaccuracies, is again to forget that in entering the world, God's word must speak through human minds. Another common instance of idolatry within Protestantism has been the deification of private religious experience. The Protestant Church's insistence that faith must be a living experience has often led its constituents to assume that any vital experience must be the working of the Holy Spirit. Perhaps so, but again the experience is never pure Spirit. The Spirit must assume the contours of the human vessel, which means again that the whole is never uncompounded.

By rejecting all such absolutes, Protestantism tries to keep faith with the first commandment, "You shall have no other gods before me." The injunction contains a negative, and for many the word "Protestant" too carries a predominantly negative ring. Is not a Protestant a person who protests *against* something? We have seen that this is certainly true; Protestants who are truly such protest without ceasing the usurpation of God's place by anything less than God. But the Protestant Principle can just as well be put positively, which is how it should be put if its full import is to be appropriated. It protests *against* idolatry because it testifies *for* (pro-testant = one who testifies for) God's sovereignty in human life.

But how is God to enter human life? To insist that God cannot be equated with anything in this tangible, visible world leaves people at sea in God's ocean. God doubtless surrounds us; but to gain access to human awareness, divinity needs to be condensed and focused.

This is where, for Protestants, the Bible figures. In its account of God's working through Israel, through Christ, and through the early church, we find the clearest picture of God's great goodness and see how human beings may find new life in fellowship with the Divine. In this sense the Bible is, for Protestants, ultimate. But note with care the sense in which this is so: it is ultimate in the sense that when human beings read this record of God's grace with true openness and longing for God, God stands at the supreme intersection between the Divine and the human. There, more than anywhere else in the world of time and space, people have the prospect of catching, not with their minds alone but with their whole beings, the truth about God and the relation in which God stands to their lives. No derivative interpretation by councils, peoples, or theologians can replace or equal this. The word of God must speak to each individual soul directly. It is this that accounts for the Protestant emphasis on the Bible as the *living* word of God.

Is not this concept of Christianity freighted with danger? Protestants readily admit that it is. First, there is the danger of misconstruing God's word. If, as the Protestant Principle insists, all things human are imperfect, does it not follow that each individual's vision of God must at least be limited and possibly be quite erroneous? It does. Protestants not only admits this; they insist on it. But as the fact happens to be true, how much better to recognize it and open the door to the corrections of the Holy Spirit working through other minds than to saddle Christendom with what is in fact limited truth masquerading as finality. As Jesus himself says, "I still have many things to say to you, but you cannot bear them now. When the Spirit of truth comes, he will guide you into all the truth." One very important reason for restricting loyalty to the never-fully-comprehensible transcendent God is to keep the future open.

The other danger is that Christians will derive different truths from the Bible. The nine hundred–odd denominations of Protestantism in the United States alone prove not only that this danger exists, but that it could conceivably slope toward complete individualism. Protestantism admits this, but adds three points:

- First, Protestant diversity is not as great as its hundreds of denominations (most of them more adequately termed *sects*) suggest. Most of these are of negligible size. Actually, 85 percent of all Protestants belong to twelve denominations. Considering the freedom of belief that Protestantism affirms in principle, the wonder lies not in its diversity but in the extent to which Protestants have managed to stay together.

- Second, Protestant divisions reflect differing national origins in Europe and differing social groupings in the United States more than they do differing theologies.

- The third point, however, is the most important. Who is to say that diversity is bad? People differ, and historical circumstances too can occasion life-affecting differences that must be taken seriously: "New occasions teach new duties"—Protestants believe that life and history are too fluid to allow God's redeeming word to be enclosed in a single form, whether it be doctrinal *or* institutional. They are concerned about the brokenness of Christ's "Body" and take steps to mend differences that are no longer meaningful; this is the so-called ecumenical movement, which is vigorous. But they do not believe that people should cuddle up to one another just to keep warm. Comforts of togetherness should not lead to structures that will restrict the dynamic character of God's continuing revelation. "The Spirit bloweth where it listeth."

Protestants acknowledge, then, that their perspective is fraught with dangers—the danger of uncertainty as individuals wrestle inwardly (and at times in what seems like a frightening aloneness) to try to determine whether they have heard God's will correctly; the danger of schism as Christians find themselves apprehending God's will diversely. But they accept these dangers because, risk for risk, they prefer their precarious freedom to the security of doctrines or institutions that (even while looking toward God) remain fallible. It is their faith that, in the end, prevents these burdens from discouraging them.

Asked where he would stand if the Catholic Church excommunicated him, Luther is said to have replied, "Under the sky."

CODA

One of life's quiet excitements is to stand somewhat to one side and watch yourself softly become the author of something beautiful. I experienced that excitement often in writing this book. The first and last days of 2004 stand like bookends, for the writing of the book took almost exactly that long and it was the most exciting writing year of my life. It is easy to say why.

One of my undergraduate students went on to become a world-class astronomer who designed the light shows for the Adler Planetarium in Chicago. Now retired, he tells me he still gets excited when the current issue of *Astronomy* arrives. He hurries to his desk and on opening it says to himself, "Let's see what astonishing discovery was made this month." I understand that completely, for it was with something of that feeling that I turned to my computer each morning, wondering what excitement was going to fall into my lap that day. More days than not something did, and it would feel as if it had dropped into my lap from heaven.

For example, there was the morning when a former student told me of the tears he found streaming down his cheeks when he read Plato's Allegory of the Cave for the first time. That became the Prologue of this book.

There were the several weeks during which modernity's mistake (with its disastrous consequences for the human spirit) came into clear focus. I had been dealing with that mistake for decades, but only then could I condense it into a single sentence. Its mistake, I saw, was its inability to distinguish absence-of-evidence from evidence-of-absence. Alternatively stated, I saw that it failed to see that the fact that science cannot get its hands on supernatural things such as God is no proof that they don't exist. That became the Introduction.

Next came the realization that there is a worldview that all religions share, a "universal grammar of religion" that parallels Noam Chomsky's discovery of the universal depth grammar that sets the rules for all human languages. Describing the specifics of that universal worldview as it surfaces in Christianity became Part One of this book, "The Christian Worldview." Working it out caused its jigsaw pieces to stand out in clear relief. To cite only one example, to do justice to its subject, religion requires a technical language that parallels the technical language of science, which is mathematics. The technical language of religion is symbolism, with storytelling one of its most important varieties. And there was the title for Part Two, the central chapter of my book: "The Christian Story."

Coda

As I got into writing that Christian story, my excitement kept gathering momentum. I came to appreciate the sheer capaciousness of the mind's of the theologians who carved out the contours of Christian theology, and also how well equipped I was to be a Christian storyteller.

In our missionary home in traditional China, breakfast was followed by morning prayers, which included our servants' family. As we sat in a circle, our mother would lead us in singing a stanza of a hymn, in Chinese, of course. Then adults would take turns reading the verses of a chapter in the Bible, with our cook helping them when characters were stumbled over. Then we would stand, about face, get down on our knees, and bury our faces in our hands on the seats of our chairs as my father led us in a prayer that closed with all of us saying the Lord's Prayer. That prayer still trips off my tongue as easily in Chinese as in English.

Not many Christians today have been blessed by being as indelibly imprinted by Christianity as I have, and it prepared me to tell the Christian story from the inside. When I would take a midmorning coffee break, more often than not I would find myself singing lines from hymns in which the ideas I was writing about would burst into song. And I seldom had to reach for my Bible to check my quotations, for they were in my head and in my life.

That is the story behind the Christian story I have written.

Huston Smith
Berkeley, California

ACKNOWLEDGMENTS

My chief debt is to my parents who, in a close-knit missionary family in rural China, instilled in me a Christianity that was able to withstand the dominating secular culture of modernity and emerge with this book.

What I learned from my teachers, among whom I include many of my students, is so much a part of my thinking that I cannot factor it out, but I know that it is a very great deal. James Cutsinger's *Not of This World* has been within arm's reach throughout the writing of this book, and many of my book's quotations are drawn from that anthology of Christian mysticism. Robin Griffith-Jones's *The Gospel According to Paul* was invaluable while I was writing the section on that great saint. Raymond Gawronski, a former student of mine, helped me so much with the section on Roman Catholicism in Part Three of this book that he should be considered its originating coauthor. I hate to think of the book I would have published if the aforementioned James Cutsinger had not gone over my final draft with a fine-tooth comb and corrected innumerable mistakes.

Authors' thanks to their editors are often perfunctory, but mine is a special case that occasions this lengthier tribute. John Loudon has been more than my editor. Ever since, back in the 1970s, *Parabola* commissioned him to interview me for the first in its series of profiles and he came to Syracuse and I ended up inviting him to stay overnight because we found each other interesting, he has been my friend.

I have the following account from Clayton Carlson, whom Harper sent from its New York office to found HarperSan-Francisco. It was part of his job to keep his eye on book reviews, and John Loudon's name kept turning up. His reviews were consistently outstanding; they were discerning, and when they damned the books Clayton was publishing, Clayton came to see that he was right. So there came a day, Clayton told me, when he found himself saying, "I'd better get this man on my side." So he hired John, and (it is hardly too much to say) John took me to HarperSanFrancisco with him. He has shepherded me through most of the books I have published since then, and Clayton was right. He has good judgment, and is in my case a good friend.

It is synchronous, therefore, that with his transition from HarperSanFrancisco to a new independent editing and writing career, this may be the last book on religion I will write. One on philosophy is waiting in the wings, but time holds the key to that one.

To all of the above, my sincerest thanks.

INDEX

Abhishiktananda (Benedictine monk turned Vedantist), 15

Abraham, 95

Adam and Eve, 10, 14, 104, 105

Adler Planetarium (Chicago), 163

alchemy, 74

Alcoholics Anonymous, 91

Allah, 12

Allegory of the Cave (Plato), 1, 164

ananda ("bliss" in Sanskrit), 73

anima (Latin for "soul"), 118

anti-Semitism, 71

ants/Ants: Native American anecdote, 24–25

Apophatic Godhead, 11

Apostles' Creed, 99, 101–102, 118

Aristotle, 19, 118

Ascension, 74–75, 132

Astronomy (journal), 163

Athos, Mount, 150–151

Atonement: doctrine of, 102–113

Augustine, St., 3, 20, 91, 96, 119

authority: differences between Orthodoxy/Catholicism on, 143–144; Roman Catholicism on, 131–137

baptism: confirmation of, 139; of Jesus Christ, 16, 39, 95; Roman Catholic sacrament of, 137–138

Barabbas, 71

beatitudes, 56

The Beauty of the Infinite (Hart), 37

Bellow, Saul, 24

Bell's Theorem, 58

Bentley, David, 37

Betjeman, John, 68

bibliolatry, 158, 159–160

Big Bang, 6

Blake, William, 2

Browne, Thomas, 10

Buddha, 49, 73, 89

Buddhism-Hinduism split, 35

Buddhism, Mahayana, 91

Buddhism, Theravada, 91

Calvin, John, 153

Campbell, Joseph, 17, 18

Catcher in the Rye (Salinger), 150

"Catholica," 141

causation: Christian worldview on top down, 6–7; science's bottom-up theory of, 6–7; virtues ascend the ladder of, 8

Chesterton, G. K., 66

"child in his or her home" analogy, 155–156

Chomsky, Noam, 34, 164

Christian church: Christ's image to symbolize the, 85; doctrines of, 97–121; *ex ecclesia nulla solis est* claim of, 87–88; great division (1054) of, 130; legally recognized by Roman Empire (313), 130;

Index

Christian church, *continued*
Paul's role in creating theology
of, 90–95. *See also* Christianity's
Great Tradition
Christian doctrines: Apostles' Creed,
99, 101–102, 118; atonement,
102–113; differences in
Orthodoxy and Catholicism on,
143–144; incarnation, 97–102; justification by faith, 153–156; life
everlasting, 117–118; regarding
hell, 119–120; resurrection of the
body, 118; the Trinity, 113–117;
virgin birth, 120–121
Christianity: claim to superiority by,
13–14; diversity of, 37–38; Jesus as
Messiah, controversy over, 34–35,
70; examples of nonexclusivism
during history of, 14–15; main
branches of, 130, 142–152
(Eastern Orthodox Church);
152–162 (Protestantism), 130–144
(Roman Catholic Church); as
Roman Empire's official religion,
130. *See also* religion
Christianity's Great Tradition: as
classical Christianity, 35. *See also*
Christian church
Christian love, 54, 81–84, 155; dis-
tinctiveness of, 83–84
Christian worldview: 1: Christian
world is Infinite, 3; 2: Infinite
includes the finite, 3–4; 3: finite
world's contents are hierarchically ordered, 5; 4: causation is
from the top down, 6–7; 5:
Infinite split into multiplicity,
7–8; 6: virtues ascend the causal
ladder, 8; 7: absolute perfection
reigns and problem of evil, 8–9;
8: everything that is outside us is

also inside us, 10–11; 9: we cannot know the Infinite, except as
it reveals itself to us, 12; 10:
revelation is multiple in both
scope/degree, 12–17; 11: science
of exegesis needed to interpret
text, 17–19; 12: literal meaning
of the scriptures, 19–26; 13:
rational and intuitive ways of
knowing, 26–28; 14: exoteric and
esoteric forms of religion, 28–31;
15: outside of Revelation we live
in darkness, 31–34; objectivity
of, 2; two-tiered background
of, 1–2
Clement of Rome, 135
Coles, Robert, 96
confession: sacrament of, 137–138
confirmation: sacrament of, 139
Confucius, 1
Constantine, Emperor, 99
Council of Nicaea (325), 99
Creed of Chalcedon, 98
the cross symbol, 110–113
crucifixion: events of the, 69–73;
seven "words" spoken by Jesus
during, 111; symbolism of the
cross, 110–113

Dante, 115
Day, Dorothy, 136
desert hermits, 147
Dickinson, Emily, 18, 127–128
Diet of Worms, 153
Dillard, Anne, 125–126
*Dionysius the Areopagite: On the
Divine Names and the Mystical
Theology* (Rolt), 10
Dionysius the Areopagite, 12, 29–30
Divine Comedy (Dante), 115
Donne, John, 74

Index

Dostoyevsky, Fyodor Mikhaylovich, 61

Eastern Orthodox Church: break with Roman Catholics forming the, 130, 142; corporate view of the Church, 145; mystical emphasis of, 146–152; similarities between Roman Catholic and, 142–144
Eckhart, Meister, 30
Ecumenical Councils, 143, 144
Edwards, Jonathan, 3, 4
ego, 80–81, 91–92. *See also* zero-ego
Einstein, Albert, 26
ekklesia, 84–85
Elijah, 40
Eliot, T. S., 80
"The Emperor Constantine" (poem by Milosz), 116–117
Enoch, 90
EPR (Einstein-Podosky-Rosen) experiment, 58
esoteric cores of religions, 28–31
Essenes, 43, 44
Esse qua esse bonum est, 7
Eucharist (Roman Catholic), 137, 138–139
Everything That Rises Must Converge (O'Connor), 8
evil: capacities for, 106–107; problem of, 9–10. *See also* sin
ex ecclesia nulla solis est, 87–88
exoteric forms, 28–31
Ezekiel, 19, 90

faith, 153–156
faith versus works, 92
the fall, 104–106
Fifth Ecumenical Council, 13
flourishing: concept of, 19

Four Horsemen of the Apocalypse, 123
Franny and Zooey (Salinger), 150
free will, 9–10

Gabriel (angel), 95
Garden of Eden, 106, 107
Garden of Gethsemane, 68–69, 70
"Gift" (poem by Milosz), 126
"gigantesque" language of Jesus, 50
God: Apostles' Creed on, 99, 101–102; on "becoming," 124; doctrine of incarnation in Christ, 97–102; Eucharist and communion with, 137, 138; exoteric and esoteric views of, 28–31; free will endowed by, 9–10; Islam's Ninety-nine Beautiful Names of, 7–8; Jesus as defining, 16; kataphatic, 11; pervasiveness of, 3–4; power of love and, 54, 81–84, 155; "the Protestant Principle" regarding idolizing human views of, 156–162; seeking and finding, 21–22; Trinitarian doctrine of, 113–117. *See also* Yahweh
Godhead: Apophatic, 11; Trinitarian doctrine of, 113–117
God's love. *See* Christian love.
Golgotha (Hill of the Skull), 71, 76
Good News, 75–84
good works: insufficiency of in Protestant view, 155
Gospels: four accounts of Jesus in the, 95; on Jesus's trial and role of Jews, 70–71
The Great Chain of Being (Lovejoy), 5
Gregory of Nazianzus, St., 146
Gregory of Nyssa, 19
Griffiths, Father Bede, 15
guilt, 80

Index

Haldane, J.B.S., 98

"hard sayings" of Jesus, 59–61

hell, 119–120

Henry VIII (King of England), 153

Herod the Great, 38

Hillel Foundation (Washington University), 34–35

Hinduism: Buddhism's split with, 35; as a wisdom tradition, 27

historical Jesus: biographical details of life, 38–39; crucifixion of, 69–73; during Holy Week, 65–69; political position of Jewish people during time of, 43–44; powers of the Spirit manifested by, 41–42; the Spirit and ministry of, 39–41; tension between Judaism and teachings of, 44–46. *See also* Jesus Christ

Holy Orders (Roman Catholic), 139

Holy Spirit, 85, 86, 87, 115, 132–133

Holy Week: the crucifixion, 69–73; Jesus returns to Jerusalem during, 65–67; Maundy Thursday, 67–68; night on the Mount of Olives, 68–69; Palm Sunday, 66–67

"The Horror of the Incarnation" (sermon title), 110

idealism/realism opposition, 2

idolatry ("the Protestant Principle's" protest against), 156–162

Ignatius of Antioch, 112

imago Dei, 120

incarnation: doctrine of, 97–102

indulgences: Protestant protest against, 154

Infinite: Christian world as, 3; as including the finite, 3–4; splinters into multiplicity, 7–8

intuitive knowledge, 26–28

Irenaeus, Bishop, 102, 124

Isaiah, 39, 90, 102

Islam: Ninety-nine Beautiful Names of God, 7–8; pillars of, 15; as a wisdom tradition, 27

James, Apostle, 65

James, William, 40, 92

Jerusalem Temple, 139

Jesus: as authentic child of Judaism, 54; baptism of, 16, 39, 95; controversy over Messianic status of, 34–35, 70; crucifixion of, 69–73, 110–113; doctrine of Jesus as God's incarnation, 97–102; language and teachings of, 49–61; glory of his life, 61–65; God as defined by, 16; Gospels accounts of, 95; Holy Week events, 65–69; Nicene decision about, 99–100; Pentecost and Ascension of, 74–75, 76, 132–133; resurrection of, 73–74; Sermon on the Mount by, 55–57, 89, 96. *See also* historical Jesus; Mystical Body of Christ

Jesus Prayer in *The Way of a Pilgrim*, 150

Jesus's language: gigantesque style of, 50; invitational mode of, 51–52; Muscle Beach anecdote relating to, 50–51

Jesus's parables, 17, 52–53

Jewish people: anti-Semitism against, 71; charismatic healers among, 42; Gospels on Jesus's trial and role of, 70–71; political position of during time of Jesus, 43–44

Jewish sects, 43–44

John the Evangelist, 65, 121–124, 146

John of Ruysbroeck, 28, 31

Index

Joseph of Arimathea, 72
Judaism: Christianity's break with, 35; accepts but does not seek converts, 35; different sects of, 43–44; holiness code of, 44–45; Jesus as authentic child of, 54; tension between teachings of Jesus and, 44–46. *See also* Yahweh
Jung, Carl, 79
justification by faith: doctrine of in Protestantism, 153–156

kataphatic God, 11
Kierkegaard, Søren, 82, 107
Kolbe, St. Maximilian, 136
Koran, 12

Lamott, Anne, 112
Last Supper, 67–68
Lettres Provençales (Pascal), 27
Lewis, C. S., 25, 26, 29
life everlasting: doctrine of, 117–118
literalism: inadequacies of, 19–26
The Literal Meaning of Genesis (St. Augustine), 20
"Little Gidding" (Eliot), 80
logoi spermatikoi ("seed words" scattered throughout the world at large), 141
Logos ("Word" as referring to Christ), 95
The Lonely Crowd (Riesman), 49
Lord's Prayer, 56–57, 59, 61, 165
love, 54, 81–84, 155
Lovejoy, Arthur, 5
Lowell, James Russell, 76
Luther, Martin, 91, 153, 154, 162

macroworld, 20
"the magisterium of the academy," 143–144

Mahakashyapa (credited as the founder of Zen Buddhism), 73
Maharshi, Ramana (Hindu saint), 15
marriage: sacrament of, 140
Mar Toma Church (India), 130
Mary and Martha, 73
Mary (mother of Jesus), 131, 132–133, 140, 143
Mass (Roman Catholic), 138
Maundy Thursday, 67–68
medicine man: anecdote regarding Native American, 24–25
megaworld, 20, 21
Mendieta, Geronimo de, 14
Messiah, 34–35, 70
microworld, 20, 21
Milosz, Czeslaw, 2, 116, 126
modernity: mistakes of, 164
Moses, 16, 40
Mount of Olives, 68–69
Mount of Transfiguration, 65
Moyers, Bill, 18
Muhammad, 15
Murrow, Edward R., 32
Muscle Beach anecdote, 50–51
Mystical Body of Christ, 84–88, 145. *See also* Jesus Christ
mysticism: as encouraged by Eastern Orthodox Church, 146–152
myth, 17–18

Nestorians, 130
The New Yorker magazine, 150
Nicene Creed, 99, 115
Niebuhr, Reinhold, 18
Ninety-five Theses (Luther), 153
"non-local" universe, 58–59

O'Connor, Flannery, 8, 50

Index

Oppenheimer, Robert, 21, 32–33
orienting knowledge, 48
Origen, 5, 13, 17, 19

Palm Sunday, 66–67
Papacy, 134
Pascal, Blaise, 26–27
Paul: on atonement, 103; benediction of this book, 128; conversion and theology of, 17, 88–95; his experience of Christ's love, 83–84; poetic powers of, 92–94; on power made perfect in weakness, 109; on prayer, 148; "radiance" experienced by, 79; his self-condemnation, 80; on the Spirit exceeding the letter, 19. *See also* Saul of Tarsus
Peace of Augsburg, 153
Pensées (Pascal), 27
Pentecost, 74–75, 76, 132–133
perfection, 9
Peter: Mount of Transfiguration, presence on, 65; his authority in Roman Catholicism, 75, 134, 135, 136–137
Pharisees, 43, 44, 66
Philokalia ("The Love of Beauty"), 148
picometers, 20
pilgrim/pilgrimage, 147–152
"pillars of Islam," 15
Pius IX, Pope, 87–88
Plato's *Allegory of the Cave,* 1, 164
Polkinghorne, John, 73
Pontius Pilate, 69–70, 71
power of love, 54, 81–84, 155
The Power of Myth (Joseph Campbell's TV series), 18
prayer: Lord's Prayer, 56–57, 59, 61, 165; medical school professor

on power of, 57–58; Paul on unceasing, 148; in *The Way of a Pilgrim,* 149
Protestantism: absolutes rejected by, 157–159; bibliolatry within, 158, 159–160; diversity within, 160–161; examples of idolatry within, 158; justification by faith, doctrine of, 153–156; the "Protestant Principle" regarding idolatry, 156–162
Protestant Reformation, 130, 152–153

rational knowledge, 26–28
Religio Medici (Browne), 10
religion: as beginning with experience, 96–97; claim to superiority by every, 13–14; symbolism as the language of, 23, 164; William James's definition of, 40. *See also* Christianity
repentance, 108–109
resurrection: events surrounding Christ's, 73–74; preaching the good news of the, 73–84
resurrection of the body: doctrine of, 118
"The Resurrection" (poem by Donne), 74
Revelation: examples of, 16–17; as multiple in both scope and degree, 12–17; need for, 31–34
The Revelation to John, 121–124
Riesman, David, 49
"Rock of Ages" (hymn), 3, 72
Rolt, C. E., 10
Roman Catholic Church: authority of the, 131–137; Eastern Orthodox Church's break with, 130, 142; Papacy in, 134; Peter as

first Bishop of Rome, 134, 135, 136–137; Protestant Reformation's break with, 130, 152–153; sacraments of the, 137–142; Second Vatican Council (1960s), 140–141; similarities between Eastern Orthodox and, 142–144; commitment to social justice, 135–136

sacraments (Roman Catholic), 137–142
Sadducees, 43, 44
St. Vincent Millay, Edna, 27–28
Salinger, J. D., 150
sangha (monastic community in Buddhism), 89
Satan, 106–107, 108
Saul of Tarsus, 17, 88–95. *See also* Paul
Saux, Dom Henri le, 15
science: acceptance of invisible realities by modern, 41–42; bottom-up theory of causation of, 6–7; mathematics as language of, 164; "non-local" universe proven by, 58–59; three domains of size within, 20–21
Scriptures: literal meaning of the, 19–26; Protestant bibliolatry of, 158, 159–160; science of exegesis needed to interpret, 17–19
Second Vatican Council (1960s), 140–141
Seeger, Pete, 81
self-condemnation, 80
Sermon on the Mount, 55–57, 89, 96
Shakespeare, William, 65
Sheldon, William, 48
Sherrard, Philip, 104–105
siddhi, 47
Silesius, Angelus, 64

sin: baptism and forgiveness of, 137–138; the fall and, 104–106; free will and, 9–10. *See also* evil
Sinai, Mount, 16, 40, 44
sky analogy, 124–125
Smith, Wilfred Cantwell, 15
social justice, 135–136
Socrates, 49
soul (*anima*), 118
Spain (seventh to twelfth centuries), 14
Spirit: described, 40–41; powers of the, 41–42
storytelling: ants/Ants anecdote, 24–25; Jesus's parables, 17, 52–53; medicine man anecdote, 24–25; Muscle Beach anecdote, 50–51; as variety of Christian symbolism, 164–165
symbolism: of Christ's image as church, 85; of the cross, 110–113; as language of religion, 23, 164; Mystical Body of Christ symbols of, 84–88; storytelling as variety of Christian, 164–165; of Vatican City, 137
Symeon the New Theologian, 146

Tabor, Mount, 65
Tauler, John, 114
Teilhard de Chardin, Pierre, 8
Teresa, Mother, 38
theoria (knowledge derived from seeing), 27
theosis (human deification as partaking in the divine), 147
Thomas, Apostle, 130
Thomas Aquinas, St., 38, 96
Thompson, Francis, 147
throne mysticism: in Paul's conversion, 90; in Revelation to John, 121

Index

Torah, 49
Transcendence, 18
Trinity: doctrine of, 113–117
"twice-born," 92

Uzziah, King, 90

The Varieties of Religious Experience
    (James), 40, 92
Vatican City, 137
Velimirovich, St. Nicolai, 23,
    115–116
Vincent of Léins, St., 13
virgin birth: doctrine of, 120–121
Vlachos, Heirotheos, 150–152

The Way of a Pilgrim (nineteenth-
    century Russian classic), 147

Wells, H. G., 53
Wilson, Bill, 91
wisdom traditions, 27–28
Wordsworth, William, 127
Wright, N. T., 73

Yahweh, 40, 44, 74, 113. *See also*
    God; Judaism
YHWH (God's Hebrew name, with
    vowels omitted), 59

Zealots, 43
Zechariah, 95
Zen monk: anecdote regarding,
    108–109
zero-ego: equals infinity, 63. *See also*
    ego